Walking to Mojácar

# Walking to Mojácar

poems by

# Di Brandt

with french and Spanish translations by

Charles Leblanc & Ari Belathar

TURNSTONE PRESS

Turnstone Press
Artspace Building
206-100 Arthur Street
Winnipeg, MB
R3B 1H3 Canada
www.TurnstonePress.com

Turnstone Press gratefully acknowledges the assistance of the Canada Council for the Arts, the Manitoba Arts Council, the Government of Canada through the Canada Book Fund, and the Province of Manitoba through the Book Publishing Tax Credit and the Book Publisher Marketing Assistance Program.

Cover design: Jamis Paulson
Cover image: *Conflicto de intereses* ("Conflict of interests") by Israel García Montero (Madrid), www.israelgarciamontero.com.
Interior design: Sharon Caseburg
Printed and bound in Canada by Friesens for Turnstone Press.

Library and Archives Canada Cataloguing in Publication

Brandt, Di
[Walking to Mojácar. Polyglot]
    Walking to Mojácar : poems / by Di Brandt ; with French and Spanish
    translations by Charles Leblanc & Ari Belathar.

Original English text with some poems translated in French and others translated in Spanish ; translations appear on pages facing the original English.
ISBN 978-0-88801-370-5

    I. Leblanc, Charles, 1950- II. Belathar, Ari III. Title.

PS8553.R2953W35 2010          C811'.54          C2010-904968-3

**Mixed Sources**
Cert no. SW-COC-001271
© 1996 FSC
FSC

# Contents

For Niko & Yael

*Désir, désir qui sait, nous ne tirons avantage de nos ténèbres qu'à partir de quelques souverainetés véritables assorties d'invisibles flammes, d'invisibles chaînes, qui, se révélant, pas après pas, nous font briller.*

—René Char, *"La bibliothèque est en feu"*

*Desire, desire that knows, we shall not draw advantage from our shadows, except after several real, harmonious sovereignties of invisible flames, of invisible chains, which revealing themselves, step by step, make us shine.*

—René Char, "The Library is on Fire," transl. John Thompson

Walking to Mojácar

Welding and other joining procedures


Du soudage

et d'autres procédés de jonction


Translations into French by Charles Leblanc

## Nine river ghazals

1

October. The poet is dead. The leaves of Manitoba,
you gotta admire them, turn yellow, sigh once, and drop.

On the banks of the Assiniboine we sat down and wept.
Maddie, Maddie, muddy river dog. Shh, don't talk.

Tenacious little ash tree, hugging the bank.
Archeology of cars. Biology of art. Theology of scars.

My hands that used to be heartshaped fluttering leaves
have become thick roots, gnarled in soil.

Orange-streaked sunset. Calcified bones.
The flood marks of '50, '97, '05. See? Wild geese.

# Neuf ghazals pour la rivière

## 1

Octobre. Le poète est mort. Les feuilles du Manitoba,
il faut les admirer, jaunissent, soupirent une fois, et tombent.

Sur les rives de l'Assiniboine nous nous sommes assis et avons pleuré.
Maddie, Maddie, chien de rivière boueuse. Chut, ne parle pas.

Petit frêne tenace, qui embrasse la rive.
Archéologie des automobiles. Biologie de l'art. Théologie des cicatrices.

Mes mains qui étaient des feuilles flottantes en forme de cœur
sont devenues des racines épaisses, noueuses dans le sol.

Coucher de soleil strié d'orange. Os calcifiés.
Les laisses de crue de 1950, 1997, 2005. Tu vois? Des oies sauvages.

2

After the pope's visit, the river keepers went on strike
and the ferrymen got drunk. No more funerals.

So did I. The mice in the park huddled under hay.
That was the summer of the return of the dinosaurs,

roaring along the highway at full throttle,
scattering the wheat. Flap of thunderbirds in the air.

That's the thing of it, the fertilizer ends up in the river,
choking the fish. What will the lake say?

The raft trip of a lifetime, Devil's Lake to the Locks,
sweet baptism in the holy Red River.

2

Après la visite du pape, les gardiens de la rivière ont fait la grève
et les passeurs se sont soûlés. Finies les funérailles.

J'ai fait la même chose. Les souris du parc pelotonnées sous le foin.

C'était l'été du retour des dinosaures,

rugissant le long de l'autoroute à plein régime,
éparpillant le blé. Battement des ailes des oiseaux-tonnerre dans l'air.

C'est comme ça, l'engrais se retrouve dans la rivière,
étouffant les poissons. Que dira le lac?

Le voyage en radeau de toute une vie, du lac Devil's à l'écluse,
doux baptême dans la sainte rivière Rouge.

3

We shot the shaggy buffalo through the heart,
the bullet entering at an angle, just behind the shoulder.

Ask me the question. Ten cents per gopher tail.
Two dollars a mink. Every farmer's wife's ten children.

Beer bottles, chipped cups, rotting mattresses.
Wild spirit sky dance, 3 a.m., multicoloured.

Our horses were just as wild and excited
as we were, chasing the buffalo.

Those were cows that now are sludge,
bloated hides bumping against the bridge.

3

Nous avons tiré sur le bison hirsute en plein cœur,
la balle entrée de biais, juste derrière l'épaule.

Pose-moi la question. Dix sous par queue de spermophile.
Deux dollars pour un vison. Les dix enfants de toute femme de cultivateur.

Bouteilles de bière, tasses ébréchées, matelas pourris.
Danse du ciel à l'esprit sauvage, 3 h du matin, multicolore.

Nos chevaux étaient aussi sauvages et excités
que nous-mêmes, partis à la chasse au bison.

C'étaient des vaches qui sont désormais des boues,
carcasses gonflées qui se cognent contre le pont.

4

The houses of our mothers grow smaller and smaller,
diamond rings lost in the drain.

Dragon boats, flaming, tossed by wind.
The moon laughs behind the curtain.

Should we declare capitalism a crime against
the cosmos? The stars hold court.

This place where two rivers meet, smoke signals,
birchbark, carnival, touch of skin, danger.

You don't know who Gabriel Dumont was?
Slender hands flashing, Well.

4

Les maisons de nos mères rapetissent de plus en plus,
bagues de diamant perdues dans le drain.

Canots dragon, flamboyants, ballottés par le vent.
La lune rit derrière le rideau.

Devrions-nous déclarer que le capitalisme est un crime
contre le cosmos? Les étoiles ont institué un tribunal.

Cet endroit où deux rivières se rencontrent, signaux de fumée,
écorce de bouleau, carnaval, toucher de la peau, danger.

Tu ne sais pas qui était Gabriel Dumont?
Clignotement de mains gracieuses, Hé bien.

5

O thou sweet sugar beet. Diabetic kids.
Worm eaten bunkers at the end of the field.

You want to talk about human rights?
Don't put your junk in my backyard,

my backyard, my backyard.
Bags of hide in our Dachau farmyards.

Brainless chickie nobs, crafty pigoons.
Sure, it's hell to work in the abattoir, poor things,

let them drink cheap rum on weekends.
See now the scorned Furies rise out of the deep.

5

Ô toi, douce betterave à sucre. Enfants diabétiques.
Des hangars mangés par les vers à l'extrémité du champ.

Tu veux parler des droits de la personne?
Ne jette pas tes déchets dans ma cour,

mon arrière-cour, mon arrière-cour.
Sacs de carcasses dans nos fermes de Dachau.

Caboches de poulets sans cervelle, porcs transgéniques rusés.
C'est vrai. Travailler dans un abattoir, c'est l'enfer, pauvres bêtes,

laisse-les boire du rhum minable en fin de semaine.
Observe les Furies méprisées émerger des profondeurs.

6

Red and yellow, black and white.
Our mouths are full of blood: is it the blood we'll live by?

Nausea: the dance of your lost singing soul.
It's no longer a question of avoiding disaster, is it.

On Saturdays she teaches salsa, rumba, bolero,
on Sundays she rehearses despair.

When I think of Cali, I think of you, Esteban, your face
lit up, head over heels in love with your grandchild.

Which would you rather have, salsa or cars?
The veins of the earth, granite, flesh, breathing.

6

Rouge et jaune, noir et blanc.
Nos bouches sont remplies de sang : est-il celui qui nous accompagnera?

Nausée : la danse de ton âme chantante perdue.
Il ne s'agit plus d'éviter le désastre, n'est-ce pas.

Le samedi, elle enseigne la salsa, la rumba, le boléro,
le dimanche, elle répète le désespoir.

Lorsque je pense à Cali, je pense à toi, Esteban, ton visage
illuminé, éperdument amoureux de ton petit-fils.

Que préférerais-tu avoir, la salsa ou des voitures?
Les veines de la terre, granit, chair, qui respirent.

7

Pay attention, if a white horse rides into your dreams,
you will be blessed with a heroic life.

Child with no name, your shrill voice pierced me
to the quick, your 80-year-old face, raptor eyes.

Same for the elephant, the wolf, and the eagle.
Squeaky wooden wheels trampling the sweet grass.

The wonder of sea legs, in the middle of prairie.
At night we worshipped the stars, gorgeous dark

echoing in our minds, gasp of infinity.
Invasion of loosestrife, toxic algae, free trade.

Fais attention, si un cheval blanc galope dans tes rêves,
tu seras béni avec une vie héroïque.

Enfant sans nom, ta voix stridente m'a percée
jusqu'au sang, ton visage âgé de 80 ans, yeux de rapace.

De même pour l'éléphant, le loup et l'aigle.
Roues en bois grinçantes qui piétinent le foin d'odeur.

La merveille d'avoir le pied marin, au milieu des prairies.
La nuit nous rendions un culte aux étoiles, noirceur splendide

qui retentit dans nos têtes, souffle d'infini.
Invasion de dissensions vagues, algues toxiques, libre-échange.

8

The museum as mausoleum, hallmark greeting card.
Dear mom, we would have been here.

Pity citizens with oil under their houses
as the petroleum economy comes crashing down.

Could there have been another way?
Genghis Khan gallops away across Mongolia.

The  music of the spheres is out of whack,
vibrating to engine motors instead of hymns.

Sing it, little sparrow, Leonard Cohen. *From bitter
searching of the heart, we rise to play a greater part.*

8

Le musée comme un mausolée, carte de souhaits hallmark.
Chère maman, nous aurions été ici.

Aie pitié des citoyens qui ont du pétrole sous la maison
au moment où l'économie pétrolière s'écroule.

Est-ce qu'une autre voie était possible?
Gengis Khan galope à travers la Mongolie.

La musique des sphères est détraquée,
vibrant au son des moteurs au lieu des hymnes.

Chante-la, petit moineau, Leonard Cohen. *From bitter
searching of the heart, we rise to play a greater part.*

9

Kissing X was like kissing rubber. I miss your kiss,
angels ascending and descending the staircase of heaven.

There are hard times acoming, Jesus.
What are we observing if not the daily kitchen.

Now let us practise both jubilation and restraint.
I river, I river, I river.

The mice were right, hay makes the best insulation
against winter. Smells nice too.

Poor Tom's acold. *Winnipi* is furious.
We should have ta'en better care of this.

9

Embrasser X c'était embrasser du caoutchouc. Tes baisers me manquent,
anges en mouvement sur l'escalier du paradis.

Les temps difficiles s'en viennent, Jésus.
Qu'observons-nous sinon la cuisine quotidienne.

Désormais laissez-nous pratiquer l'allégresse et la retenue.
Je rivière, je rivière, je rivière.

Les souris avaient raison, le foin est le meilleur isolant
contre l'hiver. Il sent bon aussi.

Pauvre Tom a le rhume. *Winnipi* est furieuse.
Nous aurions dû en prendre mieux soin.

## Welding and other joining procedures

"That was the summer we learned about explosive welding"

Explosive welding differs from conventional welding in that the materials
to be joined do not melt on contact and their surfaces do not deform.
There are no unwelded surfaces or signs of local melting with explosive
welding. The outer layers of the two surfaces are stripped down by intense
volatile attraction, leaving virgin surfaces which can then adhere. In contrast
to conventional fusion welding, explosive welding can weld materials with
widely divergent properties, e.g. lead can be welded to steel, science to
poetry.

The bond of explosively welded materials can be tested in two ways:
destructive and non-destructive. Destructive tests include the peel test,
the bend test, the twist test, the direct tension test and the shock test.
The peel test consists of cutting a small piece out of an explosively welded
item, gripping it in a vice, or firm fist, and pummelling it with sharp cutting
instruments, chisel, pliers, harsh words, etc. The bend and twist tests
employ whatever tools are available, gossip, vague fears, angry tears.

# Du soudage et d'autres procédés de jonction

« C'était l'été où nous avons appris ce qu'était le soudage par explosion »

Le soudage par explosion diffère du soudage conventionnel en ce sens que les matériaux à lier ne fondent pas en se touchant et leurs surfaces ne se déforment pas. Il n'y a aucune surface non soudée et aucun signe de fonte locale avec le soudage par explosion. La couche extérieure des deux surfaces est dénudée par une intense attraction volatile, pour laisser deux surfaces vierges qui peuvent se coller. À l'opposé du soudage conventionnel par fusion, le soudage par explosion peut souder des matériaux qui possèdent des propriétés très divergentes : le plomb peut être soudé à l'acier et la science à la poésie.

La liaison des matériaux soudés par explosion peut être mise à l'essai de deux façons, l'une est destructive et l'autre, non destructive. Les essais destructifs comprennent le déboutonnage, l'essai de pliage, l'essai de torsion, l'essai de traction pure et l'essai de résistance aux chocs. Le déboutonnage consiste à découper un petit morceau d'un objet soudé par explosion, à l'emprisonner dans un étau ou un poing ferme et à le matraquer avec des instruments tranchants, un burin, des pinces, des mots durs, etc. Les essais de pliage et de torsion ont recours à n'importe quel outil disponible, des ragots, des peurs vagues, des larmes de colère.

The direct tension test requires a piece of the explosively welded item to be screwed into the jaws of a tension machine. A university campus or business office with disgruntled employees will do. This test is particularly severe but provides incontestable evidence of bond resistance against perpendicular tension.

The shock test is required if the explosively welded materials anticipate severe affective differences during adherence, and consists of immersion in situations of extreme contrasts in temperature, viewpoint or experience.

Non-destructive tests include the hammer test, the sweat test, and perhaps most profoundly, the ultrasonic sound test. The hammer test involves light tapping or stroking on the surface of the welded materials. A skilled operator can estimate the strength of the bond from the quality of the resonance set in motion by the taps.

L'essai de traction pure exige qu'un morceau d'un objet soudé par explosion soit vissé dans les mâchoires d'une machine pour essais de tension. Un campus universitaire ou un bureau d'affaires comptant des employés mécontents fera l'affaire. Cet essai est particulièrement difficile, mais il offre une preuve incontestable de la résistance de la liaison contre la traction transversale.

L'essai de résistance aux chocs est nécessaire si les matériaux soudés par explosion anticipent de graves différences affectives pendant leur adhérence, et elle consiste en une immersion dans des situations de contrastes prononcés sur les plans de la température, du point de vue ou de l'expérience.

Les essais non destructifs comprennent l'essai au marteau, l'essai de ressuage et peut-être plus profondément, l'essai par ultrasons. L'essai au marteau consiste à tapoter ou frapper la surface des matériaux soudés. Un opérateur compétent peut évaluer la résistance de la liaison à partir de la qualité de la résonance activée par les tapotements.

The sweat test is best used to check the edges of the explosively welded materials. A silver penetrant liquid is poured onto the skin of the explosively welded item to impregnate its finest cracks, best reviewed under cool silk sheets. Ultrasonic beams may be sent into the explosively welded items from a variety of benign sources, lasers, shooting stars, sympathetic friends.

The difference between the intensity of the intermediate and background echo of a good welded bond and the intermediate and background echo of a weak bond is striking. Hear them rippling, sparking, in every direction.

L'essai de ressuage est le plus utile pour vérifier les extrémités des matériaux soudés par explosion. Un liquide pénétrant de couleur argentée est versé sur la peau de l'objet soudé par explosion pour imprégner ses fissures les plus fines, un examen idéal sous des draps de soie frais. Des faisceaux ultrasonores peuvent être dirigés vers les objets soudés par explosion à partir d'une variété de sources anodines, lasers, étoiles filantes, amis sympathiques.

La différence entre l'intensité de l'écho intermédiaire et d'arrière-plan d'une liaison bien soudée et de l'écho intermédiaire et d'arrière-plan d'une liaison mal soudée est frappante. Écoutez-les faire des vagues, former des étincelles, dans toutes les directions.

"Or perhaps more like thermonuclear fusion"

In fission reactions, a heavy nucleus, a family, say, splits into two lighter
nuclei, through differences or marital separation, plus two or three neutrons
with high kinetic energy, house, cottage, children. In fusion reactions, two
light nuclei join to form a heavy nucleus, a household, say, and a light
nucleus with high kinetic energy, shared projects, offspring. Fission is easily
understood and widely used. Fusion is more difficult to manage, for all its
promise of ongoing useful heat.

The fundamental problem in fusing two nuclei, that is, subjects with very
different histories and life experiences, is that they are each positively
charged and so repel each other. However, if the subjects meet head on with
high enough energy, say in a busy traffic intersection, or interdisciplinary
seminar, or bar, they can get close enough to each other for the forces which
hold all nuclei together, despite their net positive charges, to overcome their
repulsion; in this way they can begin to "touch."

(Remember the word "touch" must be used loosely because nuclei don't
have clearly defined boundaries.)

« Ou peut-être davantage une fusion thermonucléaire »

Dans les réactions de fission, un noyau lourd, disons une famille, se divise en deux noyaux plus légers, en raison de différences ou d'une séparation conjugale, plus en deux ou trois neutrons ayant une énergie cinétique élevée, maison, chalet, enfants. Dans les réactions de fusion, deux noyaux légers se lient pour former un noyau lourd, disons un ménage, et un noyau léger ayant une énergie cinétique élevée, projets partagés, descendants. La fission se comprend facilement et on l'utilise couramment. La fusion est plus difficile à régir, malgré sa grande promesse de chaleur utile continue.

Le problème fondamental de la fusion de deux noyaux, c'est-à-dire des sujets ayant des histoires et des expériences de vie très différentes, est qu'ils sont tous deux chargés positivement et qu'ils se repoussent donc. Toutefois, si les sujets se rencontrent de front avec une énergie assez élevée, disons à une intersection achalandée, ou dans un séminaire interdisciplinaire, ou un bar, ils peuvent se rapprocher suffisamment l'un de l'autre pour que les forces qui permettent la cohésion de tous les noyaux, malgré leurs charges positives nettes, surmontent leur répulsion; ainsi ils peuvent commencer à « toucher ».

(Rappelez-vous que le mot « toucher » doit être utilisé de manière imprécise parce que les noyaux n'ont pas de limites clairement définies.)

We might think of achieving fusion by firing beams of charged particles, glances across rooms, email messages, project proposals, at each other. However, the probability of the particles being scattered out of the beam and lost is several thousand times greater than the probability of two nuclei fusing. The best way to prevent scattering is to confine nuclei in small chambers, coffee shops, conferences, and heat them to a high temperature, through extensive energetic conversation interspersed with delectable dining. This way the subjects are much more likely to collide and fuse.

While nuclear fusion was not regarded as economically viable in the past, given the high capital cost of building reactors capable of achieving nuclear confinement with enough density, it seems likely to become competitive in the near future. There is no theoretical possibility of nuclear excursion in a nuclear fusion reactor, as there is in a fast fission breeder. There is simply not enough fuel in it at one time to permit an "H-bomb type" explosion. The environmental dangers associated with fission fuel are also much less in the case of fusion reactions because of the significantly lower rate of radioactivity involved, such as resentments gathered over a long period of time.

Nous pouvons viser une fusion en lançant des faisceaux de particules chargées, regards échangés dans une pièce, courriels, propositions de projet, entre eux. Toutefois, la probabilité de la dispersion des particules hors du faisceau et de leur perte est des milliers de fois plus élevée que la probabilité de la fusion de deux noyaux. Le meilleur moyen de prévenir la dispersion consiste à confiner les noyaux dans de petites chambres, cafés-restaurants, conférences, et à les chauffer à une température élevée, par une conversation énergique étendue intercalée dans un repas délectable. Ainsi il est plus probable que les sujets entrent en collision et se fusionnent.

Bien que la fusion nucléaire n'ait pas été jugée économiquement viable dans le passé, étant donné le coût en capital élevé de la construction de réacteurs capables d'obtenir un confinement nucléaire avec une densité suffisante, il semble probable qu'elle deviendra concurrentielle dans un avenir proche. Il n'y a aucune possibilité théorique d'une excursion nucléaire dans un réacteur à fusion, comme c'est le cas dans un surgénérateur à fission rapide. Il n'y a tout simplement pas assez de combustible en même temps pour permettre une explosion « du genre bombe H ». Les risques environnementaux associés au combustible de fission sont également beaucoup plus faibles dans les réactions à fusion en raison de la production d'un taux de radioactivité sensiblement plus faible, comme des rancœurs accumulées pendant une longue période de temps.

We dream of the possibility of building thermonuclear fusion power reactors completely free of radioactivity. In such a reactor all fusion reactions would be precisely tuned to the moment and no negative energy leaks, no escape of destructive neutrons, would occur. If such a reactor became available, it would be the ultimate power source—practically free of energetic pollution of any kind.

Nous rêvons à la possibilité de construire des réacteurs à fusion nucléaire entièrement libres de toute radioactivité. Dans un tel réacteur, toutes les réactions de fusion seraient précisément accordées au moment présent et aucune fuite d'énergie négative, aucune fuite de neutrons destructeurs, ne se produirait. Si un tel réacteur devenait disponible, il serait la source d'énergie ultime – pratiquement libre de toute pollution énergétique.

"Or maybe mitochondrial tethering"

It turns out different biological trafficking systems use identical steps to accomplish desired mergers. These steps include what intracellular molecular fusion experts call tethering and docking.

Tethering refers to the initial attraction between a vesicle and a membrane, in you and me, and she and she. Tethering is not well understood. The vesicle is mysteriously and powerfully drawn into the membrane's orbit, radius, aura, and held there, even though they are separated by considerable distance. Experts are unable to explain tethering's nubile, numinous, nirvanic hold over organisms. Poets and lunatics, fetuses and toddlers, lovers and mothers, have lain in its arms, made their beds there, feathered, flown in its ether, forever.

« Ou peut-être un attachement mitochondrial »

Il s'avère que différents systèmes de trafic biologique passent par les mêmes étapes pour réaliser les fusions souhaitées. Ces étapes comprennent ce que les spécialistes de la fusion moléculaire intracellulaire appellent l'attachement et l'ancrage.

L'attachement fait référence à l'attraction initiale entre une vésicule et une membrane, entre toi et moi, entre elle et lui. L'attachement n'est pas très bien compris. La vésicule est mystérieusement et puissamment attirée dans l'orbite de la membrane, son rayon, son aura, et elle est retenue là, même si elles sont séparées par une distance considérable. Les experts sont incapables d'expliquer la prise nubile, numineuse et nirvanienne de l'attachement sur les organismes. Poètes et fous, fœtus et tout-petits, amants et mamans se sont couchés dans ses bras, y ont fait leur lit, allégés, flottant dans son éther, pour toujours.

Docking, or petting, is easier to document and observe. Snares (sensitive "n" factor attachment receptors) or in some cases, trap(p)s (transport protein particles) on the tethered vesicle surface combine with snares, or trap(p)s, as the case may be, on the attracting membrane. Hunter gatherer styles differ. Interactive snare and trap(p) complexes created by docking draw the membranes slowly closer, closer, closer to each other, until the bilayers fuse, overwhelmed by their close proximity and shared attachments.

While some investigators are puzzling over which particular proteins, poeticisms, qualities of eye contact, best promote membrane fusion, others are simply enjoying the resulting mitochondrial togetherness in a state of domestically inflected bliss. All that for this.

L'ancrage, ou la caresse, est plus facile à documenter et à observer. Les protéines SNARE (récepteurs sensibles au facteur N) ou, dans certains cas, les TRAPP (particules de protéines de transport) sur la surface de la vésicule attachée se combinent aux SNARE, ou aux TRAPP, selon le cas, sur la membrane attirante. Il y a plusieurs styles de chasseurs cueilleurs. Les complexes interactifs de SNARE et de TRAPP créés par l'ancrage rapprochent, rapprochent, rapprochent lentement les membranes les unes des autres, jusqu'à la fusion des bicouches, dépassées par leur proximité immédiate et leurs attachements partagés.

Bien que certains enquêteurs se demandent quelles protéines particulières, énoncés poétiques, qualités du contact visuel, favorisent le plus la fusion des membranes, d'autres apprécient simplement l'unité mitochondriale résultante dans un état de béatitude à modulation domestique. Tout ça pour en arriver là.

"At night they mused on the day mystery of how flowers eat light"

Coherent oscillations of a single excitation between an isolated atom, you dreaming of ecstasy under a full moon shining over the dark lake, and a cavity, me, walking down a treelined street across the county, aching for you, have been observed, under conditions of electronically charged correspondences through superconducting transmission line resonators.

O, but then the happy investigators found the strong coupling of photon to superconducting qubit, in the way they had previously only imagined, however tumultuously, across rustling shadowed fields, could be demonstrated in fact. And they did. And it was. Delightful feats of atomic cavity quantum electrodynamics, on sunblasted beaches with eggshaped coloured stones, beside damp wood smoky fires at sundown, under wool blankets through ecstatic starfilled nights.

« La nuit, ils méditaient sur le mystère du jour, comment les fleurs mangent la lumière »

Des oscillations cohérentes d'une seule excitation entre un atome isolé, toi qui rêve d'extase sous la pleine lune brillante sur le lac noir, et une cavité, moi, qui marche dans une rue bordée d'arbres à travers le comté, mourant d'envie de toi, ont été observées, dans des conditions de correspondances électroniquement chargées à travers des résonateurs de ligne de transport supraconductrice.

Ô, mais les joyeux enquêteurs se sont rendu compte que le puissant couplage du photon et du qubit superconducteur d'une manière qu'ils n'avaient qu'imaginée auparavant, de manière toutefois tumultueuse, bruissement dans des champs surveillés, pouvait être démontrée de fait. Et ils le firent. Et ça l'était. Joyeuses prouesses de l'électrodynamique quantique des cavités atomiques résonantes, sur des plages décapées par le soleil avec des pierres ovoïdes colorées, près des feux de bois humide qui fument au coucher du soleil, sous des couvertures de laine pendant des nuits d'extase remplies d'étoiles.

The rest of that steamy summer they explored the coherent and conditional dynamics of the coupled system. For example, probing the coupled qubit oscillator spectroscopically, they were fascinated to observe the phenomenon of rising coloured sideband resonant frequencies in relation to different pulses. An extremely high frequency excited the entangled qubits tremendously, evoking rosy hues in the sidebands. A variable frequency, on the other hand, de-excited them, resulting in shades of blue. Sometimes the coupled system fell into a mysterious in between state, simultaneously red, yet blue, for hours, days.

Occasionally, owing to unavoidable distractions in either photon or cavity, the system cooled to near ground state. The calculated transmission spectrum for thermal photons then became incompatible with the experimental data, a cause for worry which the investigators, caught up as they were by the magic spectacle of matter absorbing light, brushed aside for the time being. Bees, emissaries of the sun, urgent, tender, circling her petal tips, corollic radiance.

Le reste de cet été torride ils explorèrent la dynamique cohérente et conditionnelle du système de couplage. Par exemple, en examinant l'oscillateur du qubit couplé de manière spectroscopique, ils étaient fascinés d'observer le phénomène d'accroissement des fréquences de résonance de la bande latérale colorée en lien avec des impulsions variées. Une fréquence extrêmement élevée excitait énormément les qubits entremêlés, en évoquant des teintes rosées sur les bandes latérales. D'autre part, une fréquence variable les désexcitait, pour produire des nuances de bleu. Parfois le système couplé tombait dans un état mystérieux d'entre-deux, simultanément rouge, puis bleu, pendant des heures, des jours.

À l'occasion, en raison des distractions inévitables touchant le photon ou la cavité, le système se refroidissait jusqu'à près de l'état normal d'énergie. Le spectre de transmission calculé des photons thermiques devenait alors incompatible avec les données expérimentales, un souci que les enquêteurs, pris qu'ils étaient par le spectacle de la matière absorbant la lumière, écartèrent pour le moment. Des abeilles, émissaires du soleil, pressantes, tendres, tournaient autour des extrémités des pétales, luminance de la corolle.

"But their fantasy of supersymmetry remained elusive despite extensive high energy experimentation"

Like everyone else they knew of course about electromagnetic fluctuations caused by the dramatically different effects of weak coupling systems versus strong coupling systems. Among the billion to the billionth of hotblooded organisms in the infinitely paralleling multiverse they too had observed the breakdown of manageable calculations of musicated taut string connections as the coupling constant outgrew reasonable proportions. Well, who ever said things would stay reasonable?

Could they have, with enough fortitude or imagination, held out for the elusive M moment, with its murky mozartian promises of moonlit mountains and matriarchal marigold meadows miraged in melodious mist?

« Mais leur fantasme de super symétrie leur échappait malgré leurs très nombreuses expériences à haute énergie »

Comme tout le monde, ils connaissaient évidemment les fluctuations électromagnétiques causées par les effets spectaculairement différents des systèmes de couplage faible par rapport aux systèmes de couplage fort. Parmi le milliard à la puissance un milliard d'organismes à sang chaud dans les univers multiples au parallélisme infini ils avaient également observé l'effritement des calculs gérables des connexions musiquées entre les cordes tendues, pendant que la constante de couplage dépassait des proportions raisonnables. Hé bien, qui a déjà dit que les choses demeureraient raisonnables?

Auraient-ils pu, avec suffisamment de force d'âme ou d'imagination, tenir bon jusqu'à l'insaisissable moment M, avec ses obscures promesses mozartiennes de montagnes éclairées par la lune et de prés matriarcaux de soucis, comme un mirage dans une brume mélodieuse?

Ah, but why couldn't they get the bosons of force and fermions of matter, those devilish wayward subatomic sprites, to cooperate despite their careful ongoing compactification of undesirable spacetime dimensions? It was no longer a matter of simply choosing open or closed string configurations, O no, no, everywhere they looked, string options proliferated, like crazy cats' cradles in concentrated convicts' cells, shifting shadows on shale, eerie echoes in eleven gzillion to the gzillionth empty eggshells ...

It was the theory of everything they had chanced upon all right, but without supersymmetry, how indeed should they manage it all?

Ah, mais pourquoi ne pouvaient-ils pas obtenir que les bosons de force et les fermions de matière, ces esprits subatomiques diaboliques dévoyés, coopèrent malgré leur compactification prudente continue des dimensions indésirables de l'espace-temps? Ce n'était plus seulement une question de choisir simplement une configuration ouverte ou fermée des cordes, Ô non, non, partout où ils regardaient, les options proliféraient, comme des jeux de ficelle fous dans des cellules de détenu concentrées, déplaçant les ombres sur le shale, échos fantastiques dans onze googols à la puissance un googol coquilles d'œuf vides …

Ils venaient vraiment de trouver par hasard la théorie du tout, mais sans la super symétrie, comment pouvaient-ils réellement gérer tout ça?

# Apocalypso

Sometimes we were hanging so far off the edge
of the world, everything wavering, shuddering,

sometimes we thought we would fly through
the flat end of things into black, nothing.

That was the summer of fire, of flame, ghostly
belly dancers descending from the balustrade

in the lit up abandoned churches in their cut up
bride dresses, dancing through ash, glowing.

Sometimes we flew through the sky ropes
in our backs up to the stars, surveying the fields

of burnt grasses beside the cracked roads,
semi trucks smoking, crumpled, in the ditches.

The golden bands had melted off our chapped
hands, our jangling hearts vibrated off key,

brash, noisy wrecking machines waiting for
rain, the next earthquake, tsunami, hurricane.

The children mumbled in the psych wards,
their wrists scarred, their thin arms pocked

with needle marks, listening to pigeons. We
were counting the days to the end of the world,

wild dogs yelping on the horizon, clinging
to scripts that no longer applied, chanting them,

## Apocalypso

Parfois nous étions suspendus si loin tout au bout
du monde, tout vacillait, frémissait,

parfois nous croyions que nous pourrions voler à travers
l'extrémité plate des choses pour arriver au noir, au rien.

C'était l'été du feu, de la flamme, danseuses du ventre
fantomatiques descendant de la balustrade

dans les églises abandonnées et éclairées dans leurs robes
de mariage en pièces, dansant dans les cendres, rayonnantes.

Parfois nous volions entre les câbles tracteurs attachés
à nos dos jusqu'aux étoiles, observant les champs

d'herbe brûlée à côté des routes crevassées,
semi-remorques fumantes, déformées, dans les fossés.

Les bandes dorées s'étaient dissoutes dans nos mains
gercées, nos cœurs à vif ne vibraient pas dans le ton,

machines de démolition bruyantes et criardes en attente
de la pluie, du prochain tremblement de terre, tsunami, tornade.

Les enfants marmottaient dans les unités psychiatriques,
leurs poignets cicatrisés, leurs bras minces percés

de marques d'aiguilles, à l'écoute des pigeons. Nous
comptions les jours jusqu'à la fin du monde,

chiens sauvages jappant à l'horizon, accrochés à
des scénarios qui ne s'appliquaient plus, les chantant,

eyes closed, hands in the air. What were you
thinking, Ramón, riding your black and white

horse under my window that night, didn't you know,
didn't you know, the roof had collapsed,

the discarded baby was gasping its last breath
among the blackberries, the chickadees gone?

yeux fermés, mains dans les airs. À quoi pensais-tu,
Ramón, en selle sur ton cheval blanc et noir

sous ma fenêtre cette nuit-là, ne savais-tu pas,
ne savais-tu pas que le toit s'était effondré,

le bébé jeté au rebut prenait sa dernière respiration
au milieu des mûres sauvages, les mésanges sont-elles disparues?

If

If Ms. K
If mice
If cracks in the basement
If carp
If toxic silt
If whooping cranes
If angry river gods
If PCBs
If red dwarves
If bullets
If Madonna
If fluorescent lights
If ships
If mercury
If zebra shrimp
If sturgeon
If dioxin
If bridges
If aluminum
If *Otello*
If pulsitilla
If dolphins
If angels
If polar bears
If elephants
If elm trees
If bees

# Si

Si M^me K
Si les souris
Si les fissures au sous-sol
Si les carpes
Si le limon toxique
Si les grues blanches
Si les dieux terribles de la rivière
Si les BPC
Si les naines rouges
Si les balles
Si Madonna
Si les lampes fluorescentes
Si les navires
Si le mercure
Si la crevette zébrée
Si l'esturgeon
Si la dioxine
Si les ponts
Si l'aluminium
Si *Otello*
Si le pulsitilla
Si les dauphins
Si les anges
Si les ours polaires
Si les éléphants
Si les ormes
Si les abeilles

Optimistic thoughts on the incidence and value
of mass extinctions in the development of intelligent
life on our beautiful planet now in such dire peril

Mass extinctions tend to happen only once in 100 or 200 million years.

Not everything gets wiped out, a small remnant of plant and animal life
survives.

The earth is capable of radical renewal after nearly complete global
cataclysm in the relatively short period, geologically speaking, of
10 million years, astonishing when you think it took billions of
years to develop to that point.

The earth's magnificent renewal after cataclysm becomes the occasion
for dramatic new speciation and proliferation of never before seen
extravagant lush extraordinary life forms.

Réflexions optimistes sur les conséquences et la valeur des extinctions massives pour le développement de la vie intelligente sur notre belle planète aujourd'hui en grand péril

Les extinctions massives ont tendance à ne se produire qu'une fois toutes les 100 ou 200 millions d'années.

Tout n'est pas totalement anéanti, un petit reste de vie végétale et animale survit.

La terre est capable d'un renouvellement radical après un cataclysme mondial presque total au cours d'une courte période, du point de vue géologique, de 10 millions d'années, étonnant quand on pense que cela a pris des milliards d'années pour en arriver à ce point.

Le renouvellement magnifique de la terre après un cataclysme devient l'occasion d'une nouvelle spéciation proliférante spectaculaire de formes de vie extravagantes, luxuriantes et extraordinaires jamais observées auparavant.

The surviving remnant of animal and plant life becomes the seed for the next evolutionary leap toward more complex and conscious embodiments of being in the fragile gorgeous earthly dimension.

The evolutionary process as such doesn't seem to suffer reversals or devolution but appears rather to be greatly enhanced in abundance, creativity and learning in the richly developmental post-traumatic planetary moment. All living beings in the present time can trace their genealogies all the way back to the very beginning, the dream, the gleam that initiated everything.

Le reste survivant de vie végétale et animale devient la semence du prochain bond dans l'évolution vers des êtres incarnés plus complexes et conscients dans la dimension fragile superbe de la terre.

Le processus de l'évolution comme tel ne semble pas souffrir de revirements ou de dégénérescence mais semble plutôt enrichi grandement en termes d'abondance, de créativité et d'apprentissage dans le riche moment planétaire post-traumatique de développement. Tous les êtres vivants de l'époque actuelle peuvent retracer leurs généalogies jusqu'au tout début, le rêve, la lueur qui a tout lancé.

Our species, arising a mere eye blink ago, geologically speaking, seems to have been haunted by visions of apocalypse from the beginning.

These visions have been variously interpreted in our history as a sign of God's wrath at our species' ability to conceive of wisdom and right action without the spiritual strength to enact it except in extraordinary circumstances; as the result of cosmic misalignment, the chance collision of planetary bodies or other inexplicable singularities; as the inevitable outcome of unconscious biological processes; as a foreseeable incident in the inevitable breathing in and out of the cosmic body in whose arms we exist in our brief lives; and recently, as the result of ecocidal human greed, seen as avoidable on the one hand, given our human propensity for reflection and choice and heroism, and unavoidable on the other, given our equally strong, it seems, regressive tendencies toward passivity, self-hatred and despair.

Or is it simply that our species was lucky or unlucky enough to emerge near the end of an evolutionary phase of the planet, fast approaching the event horizon of a major planetary shift?

Or is this all part of a grand plan, or random experiment, did the pulsing earth dream our consciousness into being so we could witness the implosion of the universe together, rapidly approaching, some envision, omega to the alpha, a 3-minute implosion we can anticipate will be as rapid and dramatic as the original Big Bang?

Notre espèce, arrivée il y a à peine un clin d'œil, du point de vue géologique, semble avoir été hantée par des visions d'apocalypse dès le début.

Ces visions ont été interprétées diversement dans notre histoire comme un signe de la colère de Dieu à l'égard de la capacité de notre espèce de concevoir la sagesse et de grandes actions sans la force spirituelle nécessaire pour les adopter sauf dans des situations exceptionnelles; comme le résultat d'un désalignement cosmique, la collision accidentelle de corps planétaires ou d'autres singularités inexplicables; comme le résultat inévitable de processus biologiques inconscients; comme un incident prévisible dans l'inévitable respiration du corps cosmique dans les bras de laquelle nous existons pendant une brève vie; et récemment, comme le résultat de la cupidité humaine écocidaire, jugée évitable d'une part, étant donné notre propension humaine à la réflexion au choix et à l'héroïsme, et inévitable d'autre part, étant donné nos tendances également fortes, me semble-t-il, à la passivité, la haine de soi et le désespoir.

Ou est-ce simplement que notre espèce a été suffisamment chanceuse ou malchanceuse pour émerger près de la fin d'une étape évolutive de la planète, approchant rapidement l'horizon des événements d'un déplacement planétaire?

Ou est-ce que tout cela fait partie d'un plan grandiose, ou d'une expérience aléatoire, est-ce que la terre pulsante a rêvé notre conscience jusqu'à l'existence afin que nous puissions être témoins de l'implosion de l'univers ensemble, approchant rapidement, certains imaginent, d'oméga à alpha, une implosion de 3 minutes qui, nous le prévoyons, sera aussi rapide et spectaculaire que le Big Bang original?

According to various world sages who centuries ago predicted the end of their present age calendar in the very near future, the shift could have been, for us, a relatively painless one into a new and superior dimension of being, had we been able to focus our brilliant capacity for reflection and innovation in the direction of wisdom and love instead of focusing so imprudently on steel and speed and concrete.

Or was the speeding up part of the plan, synching us up with the earth's own inner accelerating heartbeat, in response to a divinely conceived intergalactic plan?

Selon divers sages du monde entier qui ont prédit il y a des siècles la fin du calendrier de leur époque présente dans un avenir très proche, le déplacement aurait pu être, pour nous, un mouvement relativement indolore vers une dimension d'existence nouvelle et supérieure, si nous avions pu concentrer notre brillante capacité de réflexion et d'innovation sur la voie de la sagesse et de l'amour au lieu de nous concentrer si imprudemment sur l'acier, la vitesse et le béton.

Ou est-ce que l'accélération faisait partie du plan, nous synchronisant avec le propre cœur intérieur accéléré de la terre en réaction à un plan intergalactique divinement conçu?

Last time around it was the dinosaurs who had become too big for themselves and were going around chomping everything up, and look what happened to them. And now we've resurrected them to become ferocious tree-eating machines, chomping everything up, all over again!

But a small number radically downsized, instead, into quick bright-scaled and feathered salamanders and birds, magical sprites, now darting about the earth, energizing us with their radiant flashes of fiery sparkling dance and song.

The wise industrious bees survived that cataclysm intact, though they may not be so lucky this time. Nor we, with our depleted immune systems and mixed-up intent.

La dernière fois, c'étaient les dinosaures qui avaient attrapé la grosse tête et qui dévoraient tout à belles dents, et voyez ce qui leur est arrivé. Et aujourd'hui nous les avons ressuscités pour devenir de féroces machines mangeuses d'arbres, qui dévorent tout à belles dents, encore une fois!

Mais un petit nombre d'entre eux se sont plutôt miniaturisés radicalement, pour devenir des salamandres et des oiseaux rapides aux écailles brillantes et à plumes, esprits magiques, gambadant désormais sur la terre, nous excitant avec leurs éclats rayonnants de danses et de chansons fougueuses pétillantes.

Les sages abeilles assidues ont survécu intactes au cataclysme, bien qu'elles puissent ne pas être aussi chanceuses cette fois-ci. Ni nous-mêmes, avec nos systèmes immunitaires appauvris et nos intentions embrouillées.

Every cultural tradition around the globe offers rituals of voluntary symbolic death and rebirth in order to practise the recognition of mortality as a temporary moment in the rhythmic process of recurring natality, in the gradual evolution of intelligence on earth. The experiential rigour of the ritual, involving conscious suspension of isolationism in the face of death, accompanied by powerful symbolic gestures of support and cosmic import implying transcendence of ordinary meaning in a context of divine love, often leads to a leap in spiritual wisdom and power for initiates, deployable thereafter in acts of creative expression and compassionate activism.

The ritual's attempt to enact symbolic death and rebirth on the individual and collective level in a context of loving support and cosmic import appears to be a brilliantly conceived benevolent trigger for evolutionary advancement, possibly powerful enough, were we to revive the practice of it with enough commitment, to navigate through the present shoals of extraordinary social and planetary change with grace and gestures of enlightenment.

Chaque tradition culturelle sur la planète propose des rituels de mort et de renaissance symboliques volontaires afin de pratiquer la reconnaissance de la mortalité comme un moment temporaire dans le processus rythmique de la natalité récurrente, dans l'évolution graduelle de l'intelligence sur la terre. La rigueur expérientielle du rituel, qui demande la suspension consciente de l'isolationnisme en face de la mort, accompagnée par de puissants gestes symboliques de soutien et de signification cosmique qui supposent la transcendance du sens ordinaire dans un contexte d'amour divin, se traduit souvent par un saut vers la sagesse et le pouvoir spirituels pour les initiés, déployables ensuite dans des actes d'expression créatrice et d'activisme compassionnel.

La tentative du rituel de représenter la mort et la renaissance symboliques aux niveaux individuel et collectif dans un contexte de soutien amoureux et de signification cosmique semble constituer un déclencheur bienveillant brillamment conçu pour le progrès de l'évolution, possiblement assez puissant, si nous avions ravivé sa pratique avec suffisamment d'engagement, pour naviguer entre les écueils actuels des extraordinaires changements sociaux et planétaires avec de la grâce et des gestes d'illumination.

Cultures that practise symbolic rituals of personal sacrifice and renewal, and the rigorous discipline of the vision quest with its attendant ecstasies, seem better equipped to confront the challenges of radical spiritual and biological transformation required of us in the present age, than those who believe in the substitutionary sacrifice of a single man for the whole planet in perpetuity, a "blank cheque" that permitted, as some have suggested, all manner of social and ecological ravage without accountability while at the same time multiplying suffering for the billions who were coerced into the imitation of his suffering instead of receiving alleviation for it, as in "atonement."

Cultures that revere poets and grandmothers as cultural leaders are more likely, as history shows, to cultivate the sorts of relational sensitivities and graces necessary to take care of our planetary home, so as to avoid global scale disasters of our own making, than cultures that revere inflationary techno-science and men in neckties without babysitting experience.

Les cultures qui pratiquent des rituels symboliques de sacrifice et de renouvellement personnels, et la discipline rigoureuse de la quête de la vision avec ses extases afférentes, semblent mieux équipées pour faire face aux défis de la transformation spirituelle et biologique radicale exigée de nous à l'époque actuelle, que celles qui croient dans le sacrifice subrogé d'un seul homme pour toute la planète à perpétuité, un « chèque en blanc » qui a autorisé toutes sortes de ravages sociaux et écologiques sans responsabilisation, tout en multipliant en même temps la souffrance des milliards qui ont été contraints à une imitation de sa souffrance au lieu de bénéficier d'un allègement de leur douleur, comme dans une « expiation ».

Les cultures qui vénèrent les poètes et les grands-mères comme des dirigeants culturels sont plus susceptibles, comme le montre l'histoire, de cultiver les sensibilités et grâces relationnelles nécessaires pour prendre soin de notre demeure planétaire, afin d'éviter les désastres qui sont de notre faute, que les cultures qui vénèrent la techno-science inflationniste et des hommes à cravate qui n'ont aucune expérience de la garde d'enfants.

What evolutionary seed, what legacy, do we want to leave for our descendants in the post-cataclysmic planetary renewal we can hope for in ten million years, after our beautiful, shining, turquoise and green earth mother has shaken off the toxicities of the modern era, accumulated in a few centuries but threatening the entire world as we have known it since the beginning of time? Or, if we can manage to shift into wholly new ways of being, what wishes and habits would we like to bring with us, or send forward after us, into the new dimension?

*In several millennia, when we have given rise to the Fifth Age, it will be our turn to be Ancestors. Who knows what this new age will remember of us as it tells its tales and stories to its children…*

Quelle semence évolutionnaire, quel legs, voulons-nous laisser à nos descendants au cours du renouvellement planétaire post-cataclysmique que nous pouvons espérer dans dix millions d'années, après que la terre, notre magnifique mère verte et turquoise, se sera débarrassé des terribles toxicités de l'ère moderne, accumulées pendant quelques siècles mais qui menacent le monde entier comme nous le connaissons depuis le début des temps? Ou, si nous pouvons réussir à adopter de tout nouveaux modes d'existence, quels souhaits et habitudes aimerions-nous apporter avec nous, ou transmettre à ceux qui nous suivront, dans la nouvelle dimension?

*Dans plusieurs millénaires, quand nous aurons engendré le cinquième règne, ce sera à notre tour d'être les Ancêtres. Qui sait si ce nouveau règne se souviendra de nous quant il racontera des histories et des contes de lui-même à ses enfants...*

# Here he comes

*for George Bowering, at 71*


He is driving to Mexico, hurtling 100 k between yellow
toothed burros, yanking stubble, he is flying over the city
of earthquakes & flowers, there, watch him land in the front
yard of Coatlicue counting spiders, cactus, old women
in black lace kerchiefs, young girls in their best dresses,
the blood on the dog he thought was sleeping red, green,
blue, neon, purple, he is contemplating inevitable strawberry
jam. Even now, after rows & rows of doorways, with no doors
& dusty radios on rickety shelves, he hopes for a cock crowing,
the perfect line, magenta-haired girls in tight skirts, swinging
crucified Jesús between their pointy breasts. First he wrote
a short sad book, & then another, & another, all shapes &
surprises, then a fat, funny book. He was a basketball, dancing
into the hoop of God, he was his own empty belly, captain
Vancouver, curious George, the original Adam, dad, & one
dark night on the highway just west of Winnipeg, he swallowed
a mouthful of prairie & nearly became a Mennonite. Here he
comes sailing into Carlos Fuentes Bay, with feathers, nosing
ecstatic fruit on misted cedar trees. Every morning at seven
a snowball appears melting in heaven. She is babbling in tongues,
fol de rol de roly O & he, he, he, he is listening all ears, happily
weeping bright autobiographic compostable luminous tears

# Le voici qui arrive
*pour George Bowering, à 71 ans*

Il conduit en direction de Mexico, roulant en trombe à 100 km/h entre
des baudets aux dents jaunes, arrachant le chaume, il vole au-dessus
de la cité des tremblements de terre et des fleurs, là, regardez-le atterrir
dans la cour avant de Coatlicue en comptant les araignées, les cactus, les
vieilles femmes avec leurs couvre-chefs en dentelle noire, les jeunes filles
dans leurs meilleures robes, le sang sur le chien qu'il croyait endormi, rouge,
vert, bleu, néon, pourpre, il contemple l'inévitable confiture de fraises. Même
maintenant, après des rangées et des rangées d'entrées de porte, sans
portes et postes de radio poussiéreux sur des étagères branlantes, il espère
entendre le chant d'un coq, la ligne parfaite, des filles aux cheveux magenta
dans des jupes moulantes, un Jésus crucifié ballotté entre deux seins pointus.
Premièrement il a écrit un court livre triste, puis un autre, et un autre,
foisonnant de formes et de surprises, puis un gros livre comique. Il était
un ballon de basketball, dansant jusqu'au panier de Dieu, il était son propre
ventre vide, capitaine Vancouver, Georges le petit curieux, l'Adam original,
papa, et au cours d'une nuit noire sur l'autoroute juste à l'ouest de Winnipeg,
il avala une bouchée de prairie et devint presque un Mennonite. Ici il navigue
à la voile dans la baie Carlos Fuentes, avec des plumes, reniflant les fruits
en délire sur des cèdres embrumés. Tous les matins à sept heures une boule
de neige semble fondre dans le ciel. Elle babille dans plusieurs langues,
fol de rol de roly O et lui, lui, lui, il écoute attentivement, heureux de pleurer
de brillantes larmes autobiographiques lumineuses et compostables

## Accidents, all accidents

As the elephant says
in the kids' story
who is asked to apologize
for trampling on the toys
left out in the yard
& does so most eloquently
& gracefully
gathering in his own
clumsiness & the kids'
forgetfulness in leaving
them out there & of course
the mom's & dad's
tired distractedness
putting the energetic
children to bed, I see now,
daddy, it was like
the elephant said,
accidents, all accidents,
& perhaps everything
can, after all,
be replaced or fixed

## Des accidents, tous des accidents

Comme le dit l'éléphant
dans l'histoire pour enfants
auquel on demande de s'excuser
pour avoir piétiné les jouets
laissés dans la cour
et il le fait d'une manière si éloquente
et si élégante
en tenant compte de sa propre
maladresse et de l'étourderie
des enfants qui les ont laissés dehors
et bien sûr de l'inattention fatiguée
de la mère et du père
qui couchent les enfants énergiques,
je vois maintenant, papa,
c'est comme l'éléphant le dit,
des accidents, tous des accidents,
et peut-être que tout
peut, après tout,
être remplacé ou réparé

# The Late Evening News
*for Henry Champ, November 4, 2008*


You are standing outside the gate of the big lit up
white house with its purring shiny black cars,
and men in black suits glued to walkie talkies.

Your face is shadow-dappled under red maple leaves.
You look into the camera that looks into our eyes,
our animated dinner conversations, our souls,

and tell your last big story. It is so much bigger
than can be told all at once. Its origins go back to
sunblasted Africa, seaswept islands, Chicago slums,

its reach encompasses queens and kings,
poor and rich, all the far nations of the earth.
You look over your shoulder at the crowds

gathering on Pennsylvania Avenue, this
wasn't part of the script, there are cheers erupting
and guards gathering, will there be a riot?

The newsmedia are trained to stoicism, straight
face and even voice conveying the worst news
to our intimate living rooms, as if it were fair,

as if your neutrality, and frequent heroism under
fire, could cancel out its oversize terrors, or
at the very least keep them at a safe distance.

What about joy? What about dancing in the streets
at midnight, what about a whole population
cheering the return of Quetzalcóatl,

## Les nouvelles de fin de soirée
*pour Henry Champ, 4 novembre 2008*


Tu es debout à l'extérieur du portail de la grande
maison blanche illuminée avec des autos noires brillantes
et des hommes en complet noir collés à des émetteurs-récepteurs.

Ton visage pommelé par l'ombre sous des feuilles d'érable rouges.
Tu regardes la caméra qui regarde nos yeux,
nos conversations animées à table, nos âmes,

et tu racontes ta dernière histoire importante. Elle est beaucoup trop
importante pour être racontée tout d'un coup. Ses origines remontent
à l'Afrique desséchée par le soleil, à des îles balayées par la mer,

aux taudis de Chicago, sa portée englobe reines et rois,
pauvres et riches, toutes les nations éloignées de la terre.
Tu regardes par-dessus ton épaule la foule

qui se rassemble sur Pennsylvania Avenue, cela
ne faisait pas partie du scénario, des acclamations retentissent
et des gardes se rassemblent, y aura-t-il une émeute?

Les médias d'information sont formés au stoïcisme, visage
sérieux et voix égale pour transmettre les pires nouvelles
dans nos salons intimes, comme si c'était équitable,

comme si ta neutralité, et ton héroïsme fréquent sous
le feu de l'ennemi, pouvaient annuler les terreurs surdimensionnées,
ou à tout le moins les garder à une distance sécuritaire.

Que dire de la joie? Que dire de danser dans les rues
à minuit, que dire de toute une population
qui acclame le retour de Quetzalcóatl,

bright plumed, palm graced, amidst the tilting
empire, weaving gracefully between the riot police,
happiness flowing across our cheeks like fine wine.

The script jiggles, wavers, quivers its nostrils
to this new wind, wafting in from the far horizon,
lifts its heels, flicks its mane, kicks a little.

Why not? Why not a little two-step right there
on Pennsylvania Avenue, in this bright moment,
of hope, of large historical inequities righting themselves,

this moment when old and new, black and white,
water and fire, mercy and remorse, salamanders and eagles,
stretch across the grand canyons of old wounds

to touch wingtips, fingertips? The story cannot be told
all at once. There are many new dance steps to be
learned. You told your wife this is the last story,

but the story doesn't end. The Ethiopian proprietor
of the local 7-11 and his brothers enfold you
in long bear hugs when you stop by for milk.

The gods visit us not because we have cried, but because
we have resolved, humbly, in the midst of fears, tears,
to begin again, to be always, again, beginners.

au plumet brillant, embelli d'un rameau, au milieu de l'empire
chancelant, se faufilant gracieusement entre les unités antiémeute,
la joie coulant d'une joue à l'autre comme un bon vin.

Le scénario bouge légèrement, hésite, narines frissonnantes
à ce nouveau vent, qui provient flottant de l'horizon lointain,
il soulève les talons, la main dans les cheveux, petits coups de pied.

Pourquoi pas? Pourquoi pas un petit two-step ici
dans Pennsylvania Avenue, pour ce brillant moment
d'espoir, de rectification de grandes inégalités historiques,

ce moment où ancien et nouveau, noir et blanc,
eau et feu, miséricorde et remords, salamandres et aigles,
s'étendent au-dessus des grands canyons des anciennes blessures

pour toucher les bouts d'aile, les bouts de doigt? L'histoire ne peut être
racontée tout d'un coup. Il y a de nombreux nouveaux pas de danse à
apprendre. Tu as dit à ton épouse que c'était la dernière histoire,

mais l'histoire ne se termine pas. Le propriétaire éthiopien
du dépanneur local et ses frères t'étreignent en te serrant
très fort dans leurs bras quand tu arrêtes pour acheter du lait.

Les dieux ne nous visitent pas parce que nous avons pleuré, mais
parce que nous avons résolu, humblement, au milieu des peurs,
des larmes, de recommencer, d'être toujours, encore une fois, des débutants.

# In this Life
*for Barbara Godard, in memoriam*


In another life she lifts her
slender arms up, up, and
flies toward the stars, long
silver hair streaming behind
her, diamonds glittering
across the blue black sky.

A nightingale cries.
In this life nightingales cry
all night long in the
rose trees, piercing the
withered bushes with their
song, their longing, urging
the spurt of new sap, buds,
blossoms, blush, spring.

In this life she is not so
much warrior as grandmother,
goddess, sister, queen,
smiling benignly over
her sleeping garden,
the trembling hibiscus,
lilacs, breathing,
amaryllis, alyssum,
clematis, magnolia, white
petals wavering, moonlit,
in the slight breeze.

## Dans cette vie
*À la mémoire de Barbara Godard*


Dans une autre vie, elle lève
ses bras minces, plus haut, plus haut,
et vole vers les étoiles, ses longs cheveux
argentés flottant au vent derrière
elle, des diamants scintillant
dans le ciel bleu noir.

Un rossignol pleure.
Dans cette vie les rossignols pleurent
pendant toute la nuit dans les
rosiers, en perçant les
buissons fanés avec leur
chant, leur désir, en encourageant
un regain de nouvelle sève, bourgeons,
fleurs, rougeur, printemps.

Dans cette vie elle est moins
une guerrière qu'une grand-mère,
déesse, sœur, reine,
un sourire bienveillant pour
son jardin endormi,
les hibiscus frémissants,
lilas, souffle,
amaryllis, alysson,
clématite, magnolia, pétales
blancs vacillants, éclairés par la lune,
dans la brise légère.

Scent of hydrangea
wafts through the windows
of her many mansions,
temperate, tropical,
igniting the dreams
of her thousand children,
asleep, inflaming them
with passion, poetry, love.

In this life, she is not so much
warrior as queen, there is
not a war on, neither between
rich and poor, nor women and men,
light and dark, beige and brown,
there is more a swirling,
whirling, unfurling
of the dream of beauty
and laughter, there is more
the dance of yin and yang,
as the children wake up,
one, by one, by one, by one,
a spiralling, a slow unfolding
of what is yet to come,
the hopes of the grandmothers
bearing astonishing delicious
fruit, bright blossoms,
new seeds—

L'odeur des hortensias
flotte à travers les fenêtres
de ses nombreux manoirs,
tempérée, tropicale,
allumant les rêves
de son millier d'enfants,
endormis, les enflammant
de passion, poésie, amour.

Dans cette vie elle est moins
une guerrière qu'une reine, il n'y
a pas la guerre, ni entre riches
et pauvres, ni entre femmes et hommes,
lumière et noirceur, beige et brun,
il y a plutôt un tourbillonnement,
tournoiement, déroulement
d'un rêve de beauté
et de rire, il y a plutôt
la danse du yin et du yang,
pendant que les enfants se réveillent
un, par un, par un, par un,
une spirale, un lent dépliage
de ce qui n'est pas encore arrivé,
les espoirs des grands-mères
qui portent de délicieux fruits
étonnants, des fleurs éclatantes,
de nouvelles semences –

In that other life she is
warrior as well as queen,
there is a war on, there are
many wars on. She sails
through the ranks of her
numerous armies, her women
warriors, handing them canvasses,
paintbrushes, pens, dancing
shoes, handing us tactics,
and arguments, and inspirations,
handing us blueprints
of that other life, the one
we are moving toward,
together, in whose garden
we are sleeping, perfectly,
and coming awake

Dans cette autre vie elle est une guerrière
autant qu'une reine,
il y a la guerre, il y a
plusieurs guerres. Elle navigue
à la voile dans les rangs de ses
armées nombreuses, ses guerrières,
leur distribue des toiles,
pinceaux, crayons, chaussures
de danse, nous donnant des tactiques,
et des arguments, et de l'inspiration,
nous donnant des plans détaillés
de cette autre vie, celle vers
laquelle nous nous dirigeons,
ensemble, et dans son jardin
nous dormons, parfaitement,
et nous nous réveillons

# Elegy

The stars hang particularly low,
particularly bright, on this crisp
early December evening, sparkling
up the thin frosted bare armed
shadowy ash trees, everyone
scurrying home to electric lamps
and gas fires, heading into the
long night, when you have restored
to us the meaning of the season,
bells ringing along the lit busy
streets of Brooklyn, skin remembering
the glisten of hot sun, to celebrate
the passing of a grand old queen,
immaculate mother of Africa,
Barbados, Canada, New York,
and her formidable children, dread-
locked, jazz-bejewelled, honorary
gowned, that was a gorgeous
lived life, of heroic engagements
and delicious digressions, Gladys
Irene, and these are tears of
happiness from the flower bearing
avenue lined multitudes, bon voyage,
good job, mum, long live the queen

# Élégie

Les étoiles sont particulièrement basses,
particulièrement brillantes, en cette soirée
fraîche du début de décembre, faisant
scintiller les minces branches nues et
givrées des frênes sombres, chacun
se précipite à la maison vers les lampes électriques
et le chauffage au gaz, pour entreprendre la
longue nuit, pendant laquelle tu as restauré
pour nous le sens de la saison,
le son des cloches dans les rues achalandées
et illuminées de Brooklyn, le souvenir miroitant
du soleil chaud sur la peau, pour célébrer
le passage d'une grande reine âgée,
mère immaculée de l'Afrique,
de la Barbade, du Canada, de New York,
et ses enfants formidables, avec leurs tresses
rastas, parés de bijoux jazz, portant
des vêtements honorifiques, ce fut une vie
splendide de missions héroïques et
de digressions délicieuses, Gladys
Irene, et ce sont des larmes de bonheur
que pleurent les multitudes qui bordent
l'avenue en portant des fleurs, bon voyage,
bon travail, maman, vive la reine

# Prayer for my goddaughter

*for Ilce, at age 15*

And now here you are,
poised with such grace
at the edge of the world,

your tender shooted
girlhood, your jade-
scented heritage held

firmly in your left hand,
your flowering womanhood,
your star-touched future

sparkling, like blue
butterflies unfolding
their new bright wings

on the edge of the forest,
ready to take flight,
moving into the day,

sun flashing proudly,
turquoise and silver clad,
in your right. I wish for you

dear daughter, *sobrina,*
*amiga,* blue skies
and gentle winds, songs

that will move hearts
and inspire trees
to dance with you,

## Prière pour ma filleule
*pour Ilce, à 15 ans*

Et maintenant tu es ici,
prête à tout si gracieuse
au bout du monde,

ton enfance bourgeonnante,
ton patrimoine de jade
parfumé que tu tiens

fermement dans la main gauche,
ta féminité en fleurs,
ton avenir étincelant

béni par les étoiles, comme
des papillons bleus qui déplient
leurs nouvelles ailes éclatantes

à la bordure de la forêt,
prêts à prendre leur envol,
en avançant dans le jour,

les fiers éclats du soleil,
turquoise et plaqué d'argent,
pour ton droit. Je te souhaite

chère fille, *sobrina*,
*amiga*, un ciel bleu
et des vents doux, des chansons

pour émouvoir les cœurs
et inspirer les arbres
à danser avec toi,

full branches swaying,
soft shoes, strong arms,
*romanticismo, aventura,*

*alegría,* the smile of the gods
on you, *mucho cariño,*
*mucha claridad.*

branches fournies qui oscillent,
souliers mous, bras puissants,
*romanticismo, aventura,*

*alegría,* le sourire des dieux
pour toi, *mucho cariño,*
*mucha claridad.*

Hymns for Detroit


Trans(e)lations

of traditional German Mennonite hymns

## Hymns for Detroit

1

Now the forest sleeps
Behind barbed wire gates,
Dogs on sofas, crows in the fields.
Michigan boys puke
In the parking lots.
Professors count grades.
The border is on orange alert.
Somewhere above the green
Fluorescent smog chromed stars
Shimmer.  See!  All around us
Flash invisible silver shields.

Another day is gone.
Night rushes in for her shift.
Nurse, give me the blue,
The purple pill
To take me far away
So I can come
Apart and back together,
With no one watching.

Da moon, da moon, da moon
Shines on us, our closed eyes,
Wet faces, clenched heart muscles,
The I75, our lost nieces,
The Afghanis and their stones.

## Mennonitische geistliche Lieder

1

Nun ruhen alle Wälder,
Vieh, Menschen, Städt und Felder,
Es schläft die ganze Welt;
Ihr aber, meine Sinnen,
Auf, auf! Ihr sollt beginnen,
Was eurem Schöpfer wohlgefällt.
Auch euch, ihr meine Lieben,
Soll heute nicht betrüben
Ein Unfall noch Gefahr;
Gott laß euch selig schlafen,
Stell euch die güldnen Waffen
Ums Bett und seiner Engel Schar!

So fliehen unsre Tage hin!
Auch dieser ist nicht mehr.
Die Nacht, der Müden Trösterin,
Eilt wieder zu uns her.
Dir übergeb ich voll Vertraun
Mich auch in dieser Nacht;
Und wovor sollte mir denn graun?
Mich schützet Deine Macht.

Müde bin ich, geh zur Ruh,
Schließe meine Augen zu;
Vater, laß die Augen Dein
Über meinem Bette sein.

2

Dawn is a frizzy fiction, pale orange,
Waking to broad noon
After the too short noisy night.
The alarm clock invented the day.

A single star watched over us.
Sparrows jabber behind glass.
Turn down the radio.
Praise the street.

2

Wach auf, mein Herz, und singe
Dem Schöpfer aller Dinge;
Dem Geber aller Güter,
Dem frommen Menschenhüter!

Dein treues Aug hat mich bewacht,
Und Deine Liebeshand
Hat allen Schaden dieser Nacht
Von mir hinweggewandt.

3

Weeds and grasses
Along the tracks
Whisper in the hot wind:
The children please her,
Tell them,
Their socks and shoes
Crumpled
Under the monkey bars.

Those were lucky lambs
Gambolling in wild meadows
Beside clear river water.
The air is too thick here
For our little lungs,
Each morning we wake
Coughing and reach
For our puffers.
Big trucks drive by
On big noisy wheels.
Jesus saves.
Mummy said don't eat
The fish,
Watch them on TV.

3

Aus dem Himmel ferne,
Wo die Englein sind,
Schaut doch Gott so gerne
Her auf jedes Kind.
Sagt's den Kindern allen,
Daß ein Vater ist,
Dem sie wohlgefallen,
Der sie nie vergißt.

Weil ich Jesu Schäflein bin,
Freu ich mich nur immerhin
Über meinen guten Hirten,
Der mich wohl weiß zu bewirten,
Der mich liebet, Der mich kennt,
Und bei meinem Namen nennt.

Unter seinem sanften Stab
Geh ich aus und ein und hab
Unaussprechlich süße Weide,
Daß ich keinen Mangel leide;
Und so oft ich durstig bin,
Führt Er mich
Zum Brunnquell hin.

4

The fields and ditches are bare.
Lit greenhouses: the tomatoes flourish.
Snow crusts the windshield wipers.
Black ice under the tires.
Drive into the storm.
The prettiest leaves grind into dust.
Heart stopped at 6 a.m.,
The cows calmly munching
From stainless steel bowls
Their day's allotted pellets
Of chemically enhanced corn.

*Abide with me.*
Dead crows under the maples.
Killer mosquitoes.
Our soft brains,
Faltering immune systems.
It's not meteors we fear.
Our forgotten rain dances.
The enemy is here.
The worms are laughing.
Hold my hand, dear.

Des Jahres schöner Schmuck entweicht,
Die Flur wird kahl, der Wald erbleicht,
Der Vöglein Lieder schweigen.
Ihr Gotteskinder, schweiget nicht
Und laßt hinauf zum ewgen Licht
Des Herzens Opfer steigen!
Es braust der Sturm, der Wald erkracht,
Der Wandrer eilt, um noch vor Nacht
Zu flüchten aus den Wettern.—
O Jesu, sei uns Dach und Turm,
Wenn oft des Lebens rauher Sturm
Uns will zu Boden schmettern!

Herr, bleib bei mir,
Die Sonne schon sich neigt,
Die dunkle Nacht
zur Erde niedersteigt.
Wenn Hilfe fern,
dann flieh ich,
Herr, zu dir.
Trost der Verlaßnen du,
O bleib bei mir!

5

O you beautiful wrinkled *Omas*
Looking down at us
From just above the ceiling,
Fat aging cherubs
In long brown skirts
And black crimson flowered
*Babushkas*, laughing
Today where recently you frowned,
Munching gold figs,
Telling naughty jokes,
Wailing the old wild songs,
Sweet, sweet blood, open sky,
Come back to us,
Come back to you.

5

Schönster Herr Jesu,
Herrscher aller Enden
Gottes und Mariä Sohn!
Dich will ich lieben,
Dich will ich ehren,
Du meiner Seelen
Freud und Kron.
Alle die Schönheit
Himmels und der Erden
ist gefaßt in dir allein.
Nichts soll auf Erden
mir lieber werden,
Als du, o Jesu,
Liebster mein.

6

Closer, closer, closer
I want to be, to you.
Such deliciousness
In this purgatory, if mostly
In the telephone wires.
Like God, in whose absence
We practise eternity.
One long ring, two short.
Operator.
The West Jet seat sale.
Gasoline.
Faint memory of flesh.
This flickering screen.

Skin against skin,
Dark red, all night long
Behind the woodshed,
Hotter than brimstone!
Blaze, you, you, blaze,
Light by which we shine,
Sumac, chokecherry,
Ash.

Näher, mein Gott, zu Dir,
Näher zu Dir!
Drückt mich auch Kummer hier,
Drohet man mir;
Soll doch trotz Kreuz und Pein,
Dies meine Losung sein;
Näher, mein Gott, zu Dir!
Näher zu Dir.
Bricht mir, wie Jakob dort,
Nacht auch herein,
Find ich zum Ruheort
Nur einen Stein;
Ist auch im Traume hier
Mein Sehnen für und für:
Näher, mein Gott, zu Dir!
Näher zu Dir.

Herz und Herz vereint zusammen,
Sucht in Gottes Herzen Ruh;
Lasset eure Liebesflammen
Lodern auf den Heiland zu!
Er das Haupt, wir seine Glieder;
Er das Licht und wir der Schein:
Er der Meister, wir die Brüder;
Er ist unser, wir sind sein!

If I were a magpie
With blue black white dazzling wings,
I'd cry my raucous cry and fly
To you.

Ah, but I am not, have not,
Ah, but I am not, have not
Enough feathers for even West Jet.
Not today.
So I stay all the way down here,
Remembering your sweet arms, O.

Wenn ich ein
Vöglein wär,
und auch zwei
Flügel hätt,
Flög ich zu dir.

Weil's aber nicht
kann sein,
Weil's aber nicht
kann sein,
bleib ich
allhier.

7

How I love you, how I love you,
Rising radiant from your almost death.
Here is your life newly sprung
In middle age.
Innocence after experience.
Longeth.
Seaweed in your hair.
Darling. *Your majesty.*
Clenched fist.
Music in the air.

7

Du Sonne der Gerechtigkeit,
Wie schön brichst du hervor,
Vertreibst des Todes Dunkelheit
Und steigst voll Glanz empor!

Nun aber ist die offne Gruft
Ein Ort, da Wonne schwebt,
Da Gottes Engel segnend ruft:
"Kommt, sehet,
Jesus lebt."

8

Go now, friends, and scatter
My shattered flesh
Over the blue-grey water.
Cry your raven cries
Into the deep.
Sell my charred bones
To the sand people.
Ask a high price!
Weep, weep, for
My long, short life,
So bitter and tender.
Eat, drink, this fruit,
This red wine.
The sweet hurt
Of sweet earth,
The wind's cry.
Bright-coloured spirit fish
Down under.

8

Geht nun hin und grabt mein Grab,
Denn ich bin des Wanderns müde!
Von der Erde scheid ich ab,
Denn mir ruft des Himmels Friede,
Denn mir ruft die süße Ruh
Von den Engeln droben zu.

Weinet nicht, daß ich nun will
Dieser Welt den Abschied sagen,
Daß ich aus dem Irrtum will,
Aus dem Schatten, aus den Plagen,
Aus dem Eitlen, aus dem Nichts
Hin ins Land des ewgen Lichts.

Weint nicht, mein Erlöser lebt!
Hoch vom finstern Erdenstaube,
Hell empor die Hoffnung schwebt
Und der Himmelsheld, der Glaube;
Und die ewge Liebe spricht:
Kind des Vaters, weine nicht!

9

Someday when I am big
And you are little
You will sit on my lap
And tell me this same
Story of how the bear
Lost his tail waiting
And waiting for fish
To bite under the ice
Ouch! tugging and tugging
And that tricky fox
Laughed and laughed
All the way home
And then I will hug
You and hug you
Just the way you
Are hugging me
The way you are
Hugging me now.

9

Wann ekj mol groot sie
enn du kjlien best
woascht du opp miene Schoot setten
enn mie disse selwe
Jeschicht vetalen vom Boa
woo hee sien Zoagel velua
aus hee lüad enn lüad
daut dee fesch unjrem less
bieten sullen
ooweea! hee trock enn reet
enn dee klüaka Fuchs
lacht enn lacht
gauns bott Tüs
enn dann woa etj die
enne Darms nämen
enn die hoolen enn drekjen
krajkt soo's du mie helst
soo's du mie nu helst.

10

This wild is home,
Sweet, grass, mother.
George Bush's cars
Lost on Mars.
17 realms of angels.
Monkeys wailing
In their solitary cells.
They dance on clouds
And do not beckon.
Who's that guarding
Heaven's door?

Dear friends, you know,
I'm here because of you.
Ten thousand shades of green
Under the churning sky,
And you, and you, and you.

10

This world is not my home,
I'm just a passing through,
My treasures are laid up
Somewhere beyond the blue.
The angels beckon me
From heaven's open door,
And I can't feel at home
In this world any more.

O Lord, you know,
I have no friend like you,
If heaven's not my home,
Then Lord what will I do?
The angels beckon me
From heaven's open door,
And I can't feel at home
In this world any more.

11

O sacred head, now crushed
And scorned, where
Once you were golden
And adored,
Your glowing face,
Who charmed the kings of the world,
How are you so changed!

Who gouged your eyes,
From which no light escapes now?
How are you so blanched?

Was it accident, a trick of fate,
Conspiracy, murder, revenge?
Was it the driver, the lover,
The seat belt, the wine,
The jealous ex-husband,
A secret billfold, midnight fax,
A treacherous servant,
The angry queen?

All the times they mocked you
You stayed beautiful and true,
While we, so easily distracted,
Swerved across the road.

11

O Haupt voll Blut und Wunden,
Voll Schmerz und voller Hohn!
O Haupt, zum Spott gebunden
Mit einer Dornenkron!
O Haupt, sonst schön gekrönet
Mit höchster Ehr und Zier,
Jetzt aber tief verhöhnet,
Gegrüßet seist Du mir!

Du edles Angesichte,
Davor das Reich der Welt
Erschrickt und wird zunichte,
Wie bist Du so entstellt!
Wie bist Du so erbleichet,
Wer hat Dein Augenlicht,
Dem sonst kein Licht mehr bleichet,
So schändlich zugericht't?

Nun, was Du, Herr, erduldet,
Ist alles meine Last;
Ich hab es selbst verschuldet,
Was Du getragen hast!
Schau her, hier steh ich Armer,
Der Zorn verdienet hat;
Gib mir, O mein Erbarmer,
Den Anblick Deiner Gnad.

When it's my turn to suffer,
Extremities gone cold,
Come back, dear heart,
Beloved princess, golden flame,
Show me how.

Wenn ich einmal soll scheiden,
So scheide nicht von mir;
Wenn ich den Tod soll leiden,
So tritt Du dann herfür;
Wenn mir am allerbängsten
Wird um das Herze sein,
So reiß mich aus den Ängsten
Kraft Deiner Angst und Pein.

12

O you, who
Endured the bite
Of whip and knife
And boot in the Vice
President's secret
Torture chamber,
And escaped, broken,
Turned to stone,
And wandered grief
Crazed, dazed,
Across the fields,
And arrived here
In this house,
And did not turn
To the wall to die
But began to thaw
And moan and howl
And groan,
And your friends
Arose from under
The frozen lake
And wept with you
And sang
And smashed old
Bottled glass,
And danced
On smoking coals,

12

O Du Liebe meiner Liebe,
Du erwünschte Seligkeit!
Die Du Dich aus höchstem Triebe
In das jammervolle Leid
Deines Leidens mir zu gute,
Als ein Schlachtschaf eingestellt
Und bezahlt mit Deinem Blute
Alle Missetat der Welt.

Liebe, die mit Schweiß und Tränen
An dem Ölberg sich betrübt!
Liebe, die mit Blut und Sehnen
Unaufhörlich fest geliebt!
Liebe, die den eignen Willen
In des Vaters Willen legt,
Und den Fluch der Welt zu stillen,
Treu die Last des Kreuzes trägt!

Liebe, die mit ihren Armen
Mich zuletzt umfangen wollt!
Liebe, welche mit Erbarmen
Mich so treulich und so hold
Ihrem Vater übergeben,
Die noch sterbend für mich bat,
Daß ich ewig möchte leben,
Weil mich ihr Verdienst vertrat!

And sank your grief
In loving arms,
And walked at night
Among whispering trees,
And so undid
The ancient curse
And reclaimed
The world for song,
*Du Liebe meiner Liebe,*
Sweet, Jesus, Mother,
You.

Liebe, die für mich gestorben,
Und ein immerwährend Gut
an dem Kreuzesholz erworben,
Ach, wie denk ich an Dein Blut!
Ach, wie dank ich Deinen Wunden,
Du verwundte Liebe Du!
Wenn ich in den letzten Stunden
Sanft in Deinen Armen ruh!

Walking to Mojácar


Camino a Mojácar

Translations into Spanish by Ari Belathar

## The lottery of history

I have come back
to Barcelona,
Ferran,
looking for you
among the
rough
cut stones of the
Barri Gòtic,
the shining
cafés of Gràcia.
The Ramblas sings
its many
languages.
Pickpockets dart
from stall to
stall between
fire-eaters
and green-
fingered tree-
spirits,
promoting
eternal unregulated
international
free trade.
The kohl-eyed
platform-heeled
Catalonian
rulers of the night
mingle with
the pale children
of the *nuevo rico.*

# La lotería de la historia

He vuelto
a Barcelona,
Ferran,
buscándote
entre
los ásperos
muros del
*Barri Gòtic*,
los luminosos
cafés de *Gràcia*.
Las Ramblas cantan
sus múltiples
lenguajes.
Los carteristas
se escabullen
de puesto
en puesto entre
tragafuegos
y espíritus
arbolados
de verdes dedos,
promoviendo
un eterno e informal
tratado internacional
de libre comercio.
Las reinas de la noche
catalana
con pestañas postizas
y tacones de plataforma
alternan con los pálidos hijos
del nuevo rico.

The stone steps
of the Saló
del Tinell remember,
as I do,
the velvet swish
of Inquisitors'
robes, barefoot
supplication of
the accused.
Slaughtered pork
gleams in
Turkish kiosks.
Pressed grapes
sparkle in fluted glasses.
Your uncle's
fallen soldier's blood
shimmers
with junkies'
under Gaudí's lamps
in the palm-graced
Plaça Reial.
Cristóbal Colón points across
the sea, to where
my Flemish peasant
ancestors
fleeing Russian czars
found refuge in
land newly stolen
from buffalo
and Métis.
*S'beautiful, Ferran, ¿sí?*

Los escalones de piedra
del Saló
del Tinell recuerdan,
como yo,
el terciopelo suizo
de las sotanas
de los inquisidores,
la suplica descalza
del acusado.
De los kioscos turcos
cuelgan relucientes
los cerdos
después del sacrificio.
Las uvas comprimidas centellean
en los alargados vasos de vino.
La sangre de soldado caído
de tu tío
brilla con luz trémula
entre los yonquis
bajo las lámparas de Gaudí
en la Plaça Reial,
vencida por las palmeras.
Cristóbal Colón señala un punto
al otro lado del mar
donde mis ancestros
flamencos
huyendo de los zares rusos
encontraron refugio
en la tierra
recientemente arrebatada
a búfalos y a métis.
*S'beautiful, Ferran, ¿sí?*

The lottery of
history, its precious
teeter totter,
the sea's roll
in and out, out,
the dark sexy
call
of the deep,
slight Mediterranean
breeze.
Earth's creatures
rubbing shoulders,
laced and feathered,
parading
hopefully,
flamenco rhythmed,
colourfully,
up and down.

La lotería de la
historia, con su precioso
sube-y-baja,
el mar revuelto
de dentro hacia afuera, afuera,
el oscuro y sensual
llamado
de la profunda,
y suave brisa mediterránea.
Las criaturas de la tierra,
se rozan los hombros,
entrelazadas y emplumadas
marchando coloridas,
esperanzadas,
a ritmo de flamenco,
de arriba abajo.

## Walking to Mojácar

Along the winding car-
studded
new highways
of the still rosemary-scented
Andalusian hills
the poets wander,
bewildered, out of time,
flayed
by the century's losses,
weighing heavy
on them.
Herds of invisible
sky sheep driven by wind.
On the lip of a ragged
*colina* overlooking
the sea, bright
red *canciones* spring from
jutted rock.
Not for a moment,
Federico García Lorca,
not for a moment,
dark-
eyed leopard, lovely lover,
are you alone, who
charmed
the serpents
of the Hudson River
into camellia-starred
weaving,
who wept loud and long
over the crucified
bones
of the world's tortured
boy men, racked

# Camino a Mojácar

Por las serpenteantes
autopistas
engarzadas con
autos-lentejuelas
de las colinas andaluzas
de manso olor a romero
deambulan los poetas,
desconcertados, fuera de tiempo,
hechos triza
por las pérdidas de un siglo
que pesa sobre ellos.
Invisibles rebaños
de ovejas celestiales
impulsadas por el viento.
Al borde del acantilado,
frente al mar,
brotan de las piedras
canciones rojas
resplandecientes.
Ni siquiera por un momento,
Federico García Lorca,
ni siquiera por un momento,
leopardo de ojos negros,
hermosísimo amante,
has estado solo,
tú que hechizaste a las serpientes
del río Hudson
convirtiéndolas
en camelias como estrellas
entretejidas,
tú que lloraste lágrimas de sangre
sobre los huesos crucificados
de los hombres niños
torturados del mundo

on grey steel-girded
street corners,
scattered, shivering,
on brown bombshelled
beaches.
You gave us blue fireflies
over New York.
You saw the sky flee
before the black plumes
of smoke and tumult
of windows.
You insisted on
dancing
among columns of blood.
Half the world
is sand, you said,
the other half mercury.
You were lightning, flashing,
in between.
We taste ashes
in our mouths, Federico.
The tourists
have pissed in the wells,
the olive trees are
drying up.
Fly back to us
across the implacable
Atlantic,
bring along your dark
doves, masks, roses,
little eagles.

martirizados en las esquinas
sobre grises estructuras de acero
dispersos, temblorosos
en oscuras playas
bombardeadas.
Nos diste luciérnagas azules
sobre Nueva York.
Viste al cielo huir
ante las columnas
de humo y la conmoción
de las ventanas.
No dejaste de bailar
a pesar del caudal de sangre.
Una mitad del mundo
es arena, dijiste,
la otra mitad mercurio.
Tú fuiste el relámpago, deslumbrante,
en el centro.
Nosotros tragamos ceniza, Federico.
Los turistas
han orinado en las fuentes,
los olivos se están secando.
Vuela de regreso
hacia nosotros
a través del implacable
Atlántico,
y no olvides tus palomas negras,
tus máscaras, tus rosas,
tus aguilitas.

# Turning Fifty

for *Aidan Hynes*
at *Fundación Valparaíso*


in the rosemary-scented
Valley of Paradise, ya gotta
admit, is pretty nifty.
Think of it, the wife
still luvs ya,
yuv managed to stay
out of gaol,
and the bugs, bless 'em,
ain't got ya—
well, maybe the odd
drop of blood,
piece of skin here or there,
this or that fallen hair—
but in the main,
man, you're the one,
shining, in yr prime.
So lift your glass,
and enjoy your time
in the Andalusian sun,
today, tonight,
you're the one
gods and mortals
smile upon,
sardines and goat cheese
on your bread,
Tom Waits crooning
in your head.
And now, what's this,
what's this:

## Cumpleaños cincuenta

*a Aidan Haynes*
*en la Fundación Valparaíso*

en este valle del paraíso
perfumado con romero
tienes que admitir
que está muy guay.
Piénsalo, la esposa
aún te quiere,
tú te las arreglaste
para no caer preso,
y los bichos, benditos sean,
no te picaron—
bueno excepto
por alguna gota de sangre
un pedacito de piel aquí o allá,
esto o aquello, la calvicie—
pero lo que importa,
hombre, es que eres la hostia,
brillando, en todo tu esplendor.
Así que levanta tu copa,
y disfruta tu tiempo
bajo el sol andaluz,
hoy, esta noche,
eres la hostia,
dioses y mortales
te sonríen,
queso de cabra y sardinas
sobre tu pan,
Tom Waits tararea
en tu cabeza.
Y ahora, mira, qué es esto:

the muse
in the branches
outside yr window
peering in,
flirtatiously,
hurry, lover,
the story's coming on,
let's do it, now!

las musas
entre las ramas
detrás de tu ventana,
observándote de reojo,
coquetamente,
date prisa, querido,
que la historia apenas comienza,
no hay tiempo que ¡perder!

# Rodeo

In Calgary the cowboys
clip spurs on steers,
clap on Stetsons
and play
Tame the Wild Beast.
It is a staged competition.
Both men and cattle
gave up their territories
long ago and signed
barbed wire prison camp
permits
whimsically referred to
in our history
as peace treaties.
Their fury is real;
it is prosthetically induced.
Paramedics stand
munching popcorn,
ready for rescue,
five feet away.
The children fantasize
car crashes and laser guns
in space.
Christ died for our sins.
It's a charade
of wildness and heroism
a whisper away
from the fibreglass
horses that greet
tourists in the airport,
the bright lit
predictably orchestrated
steroid-inflated ballet
of hockey arenas:

# Rodeo

En Calgary los vaqueros
entierran sus espuelas
en los volantes,
se calan el sombrero
y juegan
a Dominar a la Bestia Salvaje.
Es una competencia arreglada.
Ambos, hombre y ganado,
renunciaron tiempo atrás
a sus territorios y firmaron
permisos
para campos de concentración
con alambrado de púas
a los que la historia llama
caprichosamente:
tratados de paz.
Su furia es verdadera;
artificialmente inducida.
A cinco pies de distancia
los paramédicos degustan
absortos
sus palomitas de maíz,
listos para el rescate.
Los niños sueñan
con accidentes automovilísticos
y pistolas de rayos láser
en el espacio sideral.
Cristo murió por nuestros pecados.
Es una farsa
de salvajismo y heroísmo
susurrado a los cuatro vientos
por los caballos
de fibra de vidrio
que dan la bienvenida

modern rituals
to ease the shame
of our Puritan
conquest of
Nature without grace.
In the Hutterite colonies
thirty miles outside of town,
chickens squawk
hysterically
in their wire cages,
their necks
permanently calloused
and bleeding,
from banging against
the wires.
The decimated buffalo
herds huddle in
the corners of
newly broken farmers'
fields, docile, like cows.
Just north of Almería
in southern Spain,
in the denuded sun-
blasted
desert valleys
of the Sierra Nevada
foothills,
where the steady buzz
of cars and semis
has replaced
the ancient eerie
*cante jondo*

a los turistas en el aeropuerto,
el ballet de las arenas de hockey
inflado por esteroides
y lucecitas brillantes
predeciblemente orquestadas:
rituales modernos
para disimular
la vergüenza
de nuestra conquista puritana
y sin gracia alguna
sobre la Madre Naturaleza.
En las colonias hutteritas,
a treinta millas fuera del pueblo,
los pollos cacarean
histéricos
en sus jaulas
con el cuello eternamente
torcido y sangrando
de tanto golpear
contra los alambres.
Manadas de búfalos diezmados
se amontonan dóciles,
como vacas,
en los límites
de las nuevas granjas.
Justo al norte de Almería,
en el sur de España,
en los valles desiertos
donde el constante zumbido
de los autos y tráilers
ha reemplazado
al inquietante y ancestral
*cante jondo*

of the old weather-
beaten muleteers,
and the mighty
wild Andalusian spirit
has morphed into
condenados a un sol
inhóspito
en las faldas
de la Sierra Nevada,
a two-dimensional
steel bull with holes
for eyes, overlooking
the highway,
Moroccan migrant workers
still dizzy
from their death-
defying ride through
ferocious
midnight tropical storms
in flimsy
rubber dinghies,
mop sweaty brows
over straight
overcrowded rows
of fertilized
green leaves.
*At exactly five o'clock*
*in the afternoon,*
Muhammad al-Arabi
al Darqawi
and his brother Driss

de los infatigables
arrieros,
y el omnipotente
y salvaje espíritu
andaluz
se ha transformado
en un toro bidimensional
de acero con dos agujeros
por ojos,
que miran hacia
la autopista,
los trabajadores marroquíes
todavía mareados
por el naufragio
habiendo atravesando tormentas tropicales
de media noche
en balsas raquíticas,
se secan el sudor
de las cejas
en los estrechos
surcos repletos
de hojas verdes
fertilizadas.
*Eran las cinco en punto*
*de la tarde,*
Muhammad al-Arabi
al Darqawi
y su hermano Driss

reach out their arms
and faint, ecstatic,
heat-stricken,
into the bloated
hothouse lap
of the Tomato God.
In the centre of town,
the walls of the newly furbished
bullring
gleam and glitter.
The mayor
and his high-heeled
Moorish-looking wife
step out of their
shiny black Mercedes
to wave handkerchiefs
and weep
at the ancient
spectacle of Man
Facing Beast.
Lorca's *Lament for*
*Ignacio Sánchez Mejías*
floats through the air.
*Death pangs*
*turned the room*
*iridescent*
*at five in the afternoon.*

levantaron los brazos
y se desmayaron,
estáticos,
vencidos por el calor,
dentro del exorbitante
invernadero
regazo del Dios Tomate.
En el centro del pueblo,
las paredes restauradas
de la plaza de toros
brillan deslumbrantes.
El alcalde
y su esposa de aspecto moro
y zapatos de tacón
salen de su despampanante
mercedes negro
para agitar sus pañuelos
y llorar ante el antiguo
Espectáculo Del Hombre
Contra la Bestia.
En el aire flota
el *Llanto por*
*Ignacio Sánchez Mejías*
de Lorca.
*El cuarto*
*se irisaba de agonía*
*a las cinco*
*de la tarde.*

## Poets in New York

*for Scott Hightower & José Fernández de Albornoz*

And now here come
the beautiful
cowboys of New York,
equally at home
chasing bulls in Pamplona—
*a caso exagero*
*un poquito, chicos*—
or donning blonde
wigs and their mothers'
skirts to serve
Aunt Lily and the gathered
neighbours
at the family ranch
pancake breakfast fundraiser
for the local rodeo
in Lometa, Texas—
I kid you not.
Love among the ruins
of ancestral
paradigms, loose
stones on rough hillsides,
steep
tests of loyalty,
survival,
mourning,
walking through fire,
have made them
tough and wise.
You put the lie to
Calgary and Crawford,
*amigos.*

## Poetas en Nueva York

*a Scott Hightower & José Fernández de Albornoz*

Y ahora con ustedes
los hermosos vaqueros
de Nueva York,
tal como en casa
lidiando toros en Pamplona—
a caso exagero un poquito
chicos—
ataviados con pelucas rubias
y las faldas de mamá
para servir panqueques
a la tía Lily
y a los vecinos reunidos
en el rancho familiar
y así recaudar fondos
para el rodeo del pueblo
en Lometa, Texas—
no bromeo.
Amor entre ruinas
de ancestrales
paradigmas, piedras
sueltas en las ásperas laderas,
abrupta
prueba de fidelidad,
sobrevivencia,
duelo,
anillos de fuego,
los han hecho
rudos y sabios.
Ustedes, amigos,
desmienten
a Calgary y Crawford.

You ennoble Madrid.
You redeem the efforts
of your too
strict fathers' "tonal cruelty,
cultural condescension
and malice,"
the diminished
aspirations of your legendary
grandfathers.
You field emergency
after emergency
with grace:
I mean both the noisy
messy hospital kind
and the shy
spirit's tender awakening
to the shine of its own face,
*puede ser ruidoso*
*y mugriento también,*
*sí, amores,* lots of weather,
and also sweet, sweet,
the music of a blue guitar,
"granules of sugar
on a boy's lip,"
"murmurs of tiger and flame,"
scent of jasmine and leather.

Ennoblecen Madrid.
Redimen los esfuerzos
de sus estrictos padres,
las diminutas aspiraciones
de sus legendarios
abuelos, "*tonal cruelty,*
*cultural condescension*
*and malice.*"
Con donaire atrapan
al vuelo emergencia
tras emergencia,
me refiero a las de ambas clases:
las ruidosas y mugrientas
del hospital,
y las tímidas que despiertan
la ternura del espíritu al brillo
de su propio rostro,
que puede ser ruidoso
y mugriento también,
sí, amores, demasiados cambios de humor,
y también la dulcísima,
música de una guitarra azul,
"*granules of sugar*
*on a boy's lip,*"
"*rumores de tigre y llama,*"
perfume de jazmín, chupa
y pantalón de cuero.

## Arches and Doorways
*for Natalie Schifano*


She glimpses on the
edges of the conversation
sharp lines of light
on window sill, door lintel,
garden wall.
Now the sun moves slightly
and the light falls
more softly
on this rounded
arch, this whitewashed
stone.
See how this shadow
drifts, slowly,
gracefully, across the floor.
These are, she explains
to us in her magnificent
room filled with instruments
of every sort and period,
musical, geometrical,
molecular, medical,
agricultural, among them
maracas and planes
and horse combs,
"sacred spaces,"
usually thought of as
peripheral, in between,
but in fact, she asks,
are they not the sweetest
and most tender,
that slight fold of skin
where leg meets torso,

## Arcos y Puertas
*a Natalie Schifano*


Al filo de la conversación
ella descubre
puntiagudas líneas de luz
sobre el alféizar de la ventana,
el dintel de la puerta,
la pared del jardín.
Ahora el sol se mueve
ligeramente
y la luz cae con delicadeza,
sobre la redondez de este arco,
piedra encalada.
Mira como esta sombra
naufraga, lentamente,
con gracia, atravesando el piso.
Estos son, nos explica ella
en su magnifica habitación
llena de instrumentos
de toda clase y época,
musicales, geométricos,
moleculares, médicos,
agrícolas, entre ellos
maracas y avioncitos
y cepillos para caballos;
"lugares sagrados"
normalmente conocidos
como periféricos, de paso,
pero lo cierto es que,
pregunta ella, no son estos
los más tiernos y dulces,
ese suave doblez de la piel
donde las piernas

that soft wrinkle
between breast and throat,
that gentle crease
where head greets neck.
Border spaces, spaces
of leaning, conversion,
joining, pleasure.
There is no end to her
investigations,
which leap from space
to space, and measurement
to measurement,
whimsically, playfully,
with ease. God hovers
in cracks, fissures,
and slight
mistakes, often met
with groans, and
referred to as growing
pains, arthritis, coming apart.
Ah, but Natalie reminds us,
smiling benignly,
queenly, grandmotherly,
how we greet them
is our destiny,
spiritual achievement,
artistic resumé, fate.

se encuentran con el torso,
esa delicada arruga
entre el pecho y la garganta,
la gentil línea
donde la cabeza saluda al cuello.
Lugares fronterizos,
lugares donde uno se inclina,
lugares de conversión,
unión, placer.
No hay límites
ante su curiosidad
que salta de un lugar
a otro, de una dimensión a otra,
caprichosamente, jugueteando,
sin problema. Dios acecha
en las grietas, las fisuras,
y los pequeños errores,
frecuentemente terminan
en quejidos, haciéndonos
creer que no son más
que problemas de desarrollo inicial
artritis, resquebrajamiento.
Ah, pero Natalie nos recuerda,
sonriendo benignamente,
como reina, como abuela,
que la forma en que los tomamos
depende de nuestro destino,
logro espiritual,
curriculum artístico, ventura.

## Guerra y Paz

*for Israel García Montero*


And you, *el niño*,
whose Castilian parents
in a moment of
historical idealism
not unrelated to the recent
Spanish  past
named you Israel,
and cheered when their
chosen son entered
the stock market
and booed when he left it,
you move elegantly,
jaguar-like, whirling
between their
colliding wheels,
refusing to get caught.
In your green
and blue canvases
the world is desire,
is revolution,
is apocalypse,
Vicente Amigo
crooning *Mensajes*
in the background.
You are a star.
You shine between
sun and night
on the hilly horizon
of La Sierra de Gredos,
the silver-fluted
sorrow of your mother
mingling

## War and Peace

*a Israel García Montero*


Y tú, el niño,
cuyos padres catalanes
en un momento de
idealismo histórico,
no sin conexión
con el pasado reciente
de España,
te llamaron Israel,
y aplaudieron
cuando el hijo elegido entró
en la bolsa de valores
y abuchearon cuando salió,
te deslizas con donaire
como jaguar, acechando
entre las llantas
que derrapan y te golpean,
empeñado en no dejarte atrapar.
En tus lienzos verdes y azules
el mundo es deseo,
revolución,
Apocalipsis,
Vicente Amigo
tararea *Mensajes*,
como música de fondo.
Eres un lucero.
Brillas entre
el sol y la noche
sobre el horizonte
montañoso
de la Sierra de Gredos,
el dolor plateado
y aflautado
de tu madre

in your singing hands
across the mist-
shrouded *vegas* with
your father's stern
regret.
You embrace
shadow and light.
You prefer the dark
contoured colours
of grief and crimson,
hibiscus and
pomegranate,
to sharp lines of black
and white.
In your long slender
brown arms
Morocco meets Paris
and Brussels
and New York.
Bombs are falling
on Syria and Lebanon.
The stock market
is holding its breath.
The paintings in your
studio protest,
full-blooded, *con cariño*.
Your uncle stares
out of the high
window of his office
tower in Madrid
in his beautiful shoes.

se mezcla
en tus manos cantoras
a través de la niebla—
amortajando la llanura
con el severo remordimiento
de tu padre.
Abrazas tanto la sombra
como la luz.
Prefieres los tonos oscuros
hechos a la medida
del duelo y el carmesí,
flor de hibisco y
granada,
a las filosas líneas
en blanco y negro.
En tus esbeltos brazos morenos
Marruecos se encuentra con París
y Bruselas
y Nueva York.
Las bombas caen sobre Siria y Líbano.
La bolsa de valores
espera ansiosa.
Los cuadros en tu estudio
protestan con vigor, con cariño.
Tu tío se asoma
por la ventana de su oficina
desde lo alto de un edificio
en Madrid
y lleva puesto
un hermoso par de zapatitos.

## Granada

Here Our Lady of Sorrows
cradles
her lacerated son
on her star-spangled lap.
Here the baby Christ
cavorts
at the skirts of his heavenly
mother with his
angelic baby twin.
Here limps St. Roch
with his open wounds
and hound.
Here the resplendent
cunning Isabella
belatedly dubs
her most infamous
subject, mocked
and left penniless in his time,
on a marble column
in the street.
The weight of the old world
lies intricate, heavy,
on these cathedral walls,
overlaid
with stolen, melted down
Aztec gold.
On the hill above, the Alhambra
proudly remembers
the banished
glory of the medieval Moors.
The ceiling of the Sultan's
throne room
is a dome of stars.

# Granada

Aquí Nuestra Señora de los Dolores
arrulla sobre su regazo
cubierto de estrellas
a su desventurado hijo.
Aquí el niño dios
da volteretas sobre las faldas
de su celestial madre
acompañado de su angelical mellizo.
Aquí San Roque
cojea con sus heridas abiertas
y su perro de caza.
Aquí la ingeniosa y
espléndida Isabel
tardíamente
arma caballero
a su mas ínfimo
súbdito, quien fuese burlado
y arrojado sin un quinto
a la calle
sobre una columna de mármol.
La carga del viejo mundo
cae intricada, pesada,
sobre las paredes de la catedral
cubiertas con el oro
robado a los aztecas.
Colina arriba, la Alhambra
recuerda orgullosa
la desvanecida gloria
de los moros.
El techo del trono
del sultán
es un domo de estrellas.

The noble beasts
in the Court of Lions
practise elegant restraint
in their water dance
for the Sultan's magenta
silk-veiled wives.
On these intricately carved
walls is inscribed
the poetry of Paradise.
رغبـة المغـرب والشـرق
The envy of Occident
and Orient.
A crippled soldier
left behind
by Napoleon's marauding
army dismantled
the fuses of the dynamite
intended to erase these
exquisite pleasure palaces
from human view
long after Pizarro's men
across the Atlantic,
possessed by demonic fury,
burned the extensive
libraries of ancient
America and beheaded
its kings and queens.
All roads lead to Granada, ¿*sí*?
The Moor's last sigh.

Las nobles bestias
de la Corte de los Leones
practican con elegancia
el arte del comedimiento
en su danza de agua
ante las esposas del sultán,
cubiertas con velos magenta.
En estas intricadas paredes
está inscrita la poesía del paraíso.
*Raghbatal maghribi*
*wa sharq.*
La envidia de Oriente
y Occidente.
Un soldado tullido
abandonado
por el ejército invasor de Napoleón
desmanteló
la dinamita que intentaba arrebatarnos
el exquisito placer que estos palacios
dan a la vista,
mucho después de que
los hombres de Pizarro
al otro lado del Atlántico
poseídos por una furia infernal
quemasen las bibliotecas
de la ancestral América
y decapitaran a sus reyes y reinas.
Todos los caminos llevan
a Granada, ¿sí?
El último suspiro del moro.

O look, *querida,*
quick, the unrequited spirit
of a Talomecan princess
with silver earrings
and strings of pearls
passing by.

Oh mira, rápido,
querida, el espíritu, que nadie convocó
de la princesa Talomeca
con aretes de plata
y cuerdas de perlas
pasa frente a nosotras.

# I am an orphan girl
*for Carmen Isasi*


With you, *chica*, for you,
mischievous one,
*querida*, sitting in the
Plaza de San Miguel Bajo
in Granada
drinking *cerveza* in
the unforgiving Spanish sun,
I want to know Euskara,
Erditze, Egia, Etchia,
I want to find bitter oranges
and wild clover honey,
I want to recite Isabel Allende,
I want to dance *salsa*,
*bolero, merengue.*
I have no mother, no father,
no sister, no brother.
One minute you are four
years old, the next you are
a thousand.
Do we understand
one another,
do we breathe the same air,
dream the same dreams?
If you don't believe
in language, *amiga*, why
do you write poems.
And you, *chica*, why do you
stroke the beautiful paper
with your fingers,
trembling, why do you trace
the jagged lines
of the heart with graphite

# I am an orphan girl
*a Carmen Isasi*

Contigo, chica, por ti,
pícara,
querida, sentadas en la
Plaza de San Miguel Bajo
en Granada
bebiendo cerveza bajo
el despiadado sol español,
quiero aprender Euskara,
Erditze, Egia, Etchia,
quiero encontrar
naranjas amargas
y miel de trébol salvaje,
quiero recitar a Isabel Allende,
quiero bailar salsa,
bolero, merengue.
*I have no mother, no father,*
*no sister, no brother.*
Un minuto tienes cuatro años
al siguiente mil.
¿Acaso somos capaces
de comprendernos,
de respirar el mismo aire,
de soñar los mismos sueños?
Si no crees en el lenguaje, amiga,
por qué escribes poemas.
Y tú, chica, por qué hieres
el hermoso papel
con la punta de tus dedos
temblorosos,
por qué trazas con grafito
las filosas líneas del corazón
sobre seda

on silk skin
and crushed linen,
why do you not write books.
I say tomato, you say *tomate*.
We cannot talk together
but we can dance.
*Olé, olé, olé, olé, olé.*
Buffalo calls
on the Mediterranean sea.
*Olé, olé, olé, olé, olé.*
Green emeralds
and tall black rocks.
*Olé, olé, olé, olé, olé.*

y papel de lino basto,
por qué  no escribes libros.
*I say tomato, you say tomate.*
No podemos hablar
pero podemos bailar.
*Olé, olé, olé, olé, olé.*
La llamada del búfalo
en el Mar Mediterráneo.
*Olé, olé, olé, olé, olé.*
Esmeraldas verdes
y grandes piedras negras.
*Olé, olé, olé, olé, olé.*

## Divine Botany

*for J*

Let me say this, *amado mío,*
in the happiness
of my guest
residency at Casa
Valparaíso, hidden among
the neglected shimmering
desert hills
of Las Alpujarras,
where artists play like
puppies and young children,
and recite poems,
and splash
paint on each other
at midnight,
and sip *mojitos*
while the world burns,
and toast our fortune
to have stumbled, in these
cynical earnest volatile
political times,
each in our idiosyncratic
ways, confounding
teachers and textbooks,
upon the ancient mystery
of turning ordinary
metal into unworldly
laughter and embossed
and jewelled gold,
with nothing but  a turn
of phrase or gesture
of the hand, slight movement
of a sandalled foot,

## Botánica Divina
*a J.*


Permíteme que te diga esto,
amado mío,
desde la felicidad
de mi estadía
en Casa Valparaíso,
escondida entre
las abandonadas y relucientes
colinas del desierto
de Las Alpujarras,
donde los artistas juegan
como cachorritos y niños
y recitan poemas
y bromeando
se bañan con pintura
en mitad de la noche,
y beben mojitos
mientras el mundo arde,
y brindamos por la suerte
de habernos encontrado, en estos
tiempos políticos etéreos,
formales, cínicos,
cada uno con nuestro
peculiar destino a cuestas
fundando maestros
y libros de texto
sobre el ancestral misterio
de transformar metales ordinarios
en simple risa
y oro labrado,
con más nada que palabras
mágicas, un ademán,

precise graphite shading
on handmade paper,
whimsically shipped
at considerable expense
from Mexico, just so:
ah, *sí, amado mío,*
I didn't expect to
find you, floating, ghostly,
through our remote
little haven, here,
who was so dazzled by
artistic alchemy
some years ago
and thought you could
leap across your father's
iron-gated edifice
into our simple studios,
and found its spikes
too high, fatally piercing
your feet and thigh.
I didn't expect to find
you here, whimpering
like an abandoned child
among the bulrushes
in the ravine,
surrounded by
yucca and prickly pear
and soothing aloe.
Ah, but be careful,
don't you know,
that prickly-leafed
yellow plum is
*solanum sodomaeum,*

un leve movimiento
de pies descalzos,
la sombra precisa del grafito
sobre papel hecho a mano,
caprichosamente importado
a un precio excesivo
desde México, tan sólo eso:
ah, sí, amado mío,
no esperaba encontrarte aquí
flotando fantasmal en nuestro
remoto y pequeño paraíso,
tú, que hace algunos años,
te dejaste deslumbrar
por la alquimia del arte
y pensaste que podías librar
la fortaleza de hierro
que construyó tu padre
corriendo desesperado
hasta nuestros humildes talleres
tan sólo para encontrarte
con alambres de púas
lacerándote los pies.
No esperaba encontrarte
aquí, llorando
como un niño abandonado
entre los juncos del barranco,
rodeado de yuca
y espinas de peral
y la dulzura de la sábila.
Ah, pero ten cuidado,
no sabes,
que el dorado ciruelo es
*solanum sodomaeum,*

and will kill you
if you eat it for lunch.
That attractive looking
orange melon is
*coloquíntida.* One bite
will shrivel the insides
of your mouth
like a fish drinking in
the Dead Sea.
Paradise comes
with scorpions and fevers
and thorns. I forgot
you didn't know.
And poultices,
and purges,
and long long hours
of ignominy and even
insanity, clutching
a wooden spindle wheel,
teetering
on old stone steps,
fashioning invisible
sky ships of ilmenite
beaten into filaments,
quantum anti-gravity
designs,
learning to fly.
Some afternoons I see
sure-footed Sappho
clambering
up and down these hills,
collecting oregano,
composing a green lettuce

y puede matarte
si lo comes durante el almuerzo.
Aquel llamativo melón
color naranja
es una tuera.
Un sólo bocado
quemará tu boca
como pez que bebe
del Mar Muerto.
El paraíso viene repleto
de escorpiones, fiebres
y espinas. Olvidaba
que no lo sabías.
Y ungüentos,
y purgas
y largas, largas horas
de ignominia e incluso
de locura, aferrados
a una rueca
balanceándonos
sobre viejos escalones de piedra,
diseñando naves espaciales
invisibles
con filamentos de ilmenita,
ingravidez cuántica,
aprendizaje y práctica de vuelo.
Algunas tardes veo
a una Safo firme y
bien parada
arrastrándose
por estas colinas,
recogiendo orégano
preparando una ensalada de lechuga

salad for her shy
linen-skirted friend, crimson
pomegranate
blossoms in her gold-
streaked hair.
Sometimes I see you
with your crushed heart
wanting to die.
Sometimes I see bits
of your fragmented spirit
levitating, *amado mío,*
spectral,
titanium-sheathed,
above us, in the sky.

para su tímida amiga de faldas de lino,
granadas carmesí
florecen sobre su dorada
cabellera.
A veces te veo
con el corazón destrozado
esperando morir.
A veces veo los trozos
de tu espíritu,
amado mío, levitando
espectral,
cubierto de titanio,
a cielo abierto, sobre nosotros.

## The Phoenicians

In my little village
in the harsh climate
of Manitoba,
we thanked Jesus
for our food,
though I couldn't see
then what he had
to do with it,
a sandal-footed long-hair
with a gift for physio-
therapy, who liked to
hang out
with crazies and dopers
in the balmy Mediterranean
far across the Atlantic
twenty centuries ago,
and as far as I knew
never tilled a field
or hoed a row of potatoes
in his life.
Or we'd thank
the bearded Old Man
of the Sky,
who made the whole
world from a handful
of words
and got eternal credit
for this one-time poetic feat
for the crops
growing on our little
farm, like some feudal
lord whose name
appears on all
the land titles: even

## Los Fenicios

En mi pequeña aldea
bajo el crudo clima
de Manitoba,
dábamos gracias a Jesús el Nazareno
por nuestros alimentos,
aunque nunca entendí
que es lo que
tenía que ver
él en todo esto,
un chancludo de pelo largo
con cierto talento
para la fisioterapia
que gustaba de convivir
con los locos y los adictos
en el balsámico Mediterráneo
muy lejos del Atlántico
hace más de veinte siglos,
y hasta donde yo sé
jamás cultivó la tierra
ni aró surcos
para la siembra de patatas.
O dábamos gracias
al viejo barbudo de los cielos,
que de un golpe de suerte
y un puñado de palabras
creó al mundo
y consiguió fama eterna de poeta
llevándose todo el crédito
por los cultivos
de nuestra pequeña granja
como señor feudal
cuyo nombre aparece
en los títulos de propiedad:

though he'd kicked us
out of the garden
we were contracted for
in a hissy fit
and gave us weedy
fields to till
as punishment
for breaking a particular
arbitrary house rule,
and made us do
all the hard work.
Later we thought
we should
rather thank our mums
and dads,
for their extraordinary
uncomplaining joyful
labour, plowing
and seeding
and hoeing
and harvesting
and grinding
and milking
and gathering
and kneading,
and serving up
delectable meals
day in, day out,
with a flourish,
including the world's
best saskatoon and
gooseberry slice,
and we also thanked

a pesar de que en un berrinche nos corrió
a patadas del jardín
para el cual nos contrató
y nos dio
campos cubiertos de maleza
para labrar como castigo
por haber roto
una regla de la casa,
que era particularmente arbitraria
y nos forzó
a hacer el trabajo duro.
Después pensamos
que deberíamos
mejor agradecer a nuestras madres
y padres,
por su extraordinaria labor
que alegres y sin quejarse,
araban
y sembraban,
y surcaban,
y cosechaban,
y molían,
y ordeñaban,
y recogían,
y amasaban,
y servían
ostentosos,
de sol a sol,
deliciosas comidas
incluyendo
las mejores tartas de saskatoon
y grosella del mundo,
y también le dimos gracias

the queen and
the Canadian government
for letting us live
in the bountiful prairies
in peace,
neglecting to mention
the First Nations
and their wantonly
slaughtered buffalo herds
who were so drastically
cheated by our
bogus treaties and
thrown into turmoil for
showing us how.
We practised, in this way,
you might say,
the prevailing colonialist
civil labour
approach to the terrible
mystery of survival
on this dog eat dog planet,
which forces us
to occupy each other's
lands and eat
our fellow creatures
and greens
and makes eager
if squeamish killers
and invaders of us all.
It is a conundrum
that inspires children
of the glibly rich
to starve themselves

a la reina
y al gobierno canadiense
por permitirnos
vivir en paz
en estas generosas praderas,
convenientemente olvidamos
mencionar
a los pueblos originarios,
y el desdeñoso
sacrificio de manadas
de búfalos,
que fueron
drásticamente engañados
por nuestros fraudulentos tratados
y arrojados al caos
por enseñarnos el camino.
De esta manera practicamos,
podría decirse,
el prevalente
enfoque del deber cívico
colonialista
referente al terrible
misterio de sobrevivir
en este planeta de perros traga perros,
que nos fuerza a ocupar
la tierra de los unos y los otros
y devorar la flora
y la fauna
y hace de cada uno de nosotros
ansiosos y delicados
asesinos e invasores.
Enigma que inspira
a los hijos

to alarming degrees
to protect their personal
sanity against
the general lie of privilege.
In recent years we've
all been made to thank
seed companies
for giving us our seeds,
though they
didn't make
or invent or produce
them, so much as
hoard what was
freely sprouting
everywhere,
and tinkered
with it so as to
own the copyright.
Charles Olson thought,
like Columbus, that
markets were made
by the melting of metals.
Many nowadays think
they're made by machines.
But if we cut down
all the trees and burn
all the petroleum
and melt all the gold,
we would still, *compadres,*
want to eat,
and wear necklaces, no?
Who owns the world?
Who made it?

de los superfluos ricos
a matarse de hambre
para proteger su cordura
ante la gran mentira
del privilegio.
Recientemente
nos han hecho agradecer
a las compañías de semillas
por darnos nuestros granos,
aunque no hayan
creado o inventado
el producto, más bien
confiscaron lo que crecía
libremente
en todas partes
dándonos gato por liebre
como si poseyeran
los derechos de autor.
Charles Olson pensó,
como Colón,
que los mercados se sustentan
con la fundición de los metales.
Hoy en día muchos piensan
que se sustentan en las máquinas.
Pero si talamos
todos los árboles
y quemamos todo el petróleo
y fundimos todo el oro,
todavía querremos comer,
compadres,
y usar collares, ¿no?
¿Quién es el dueño del mundo?
¿Quién lo creó?

Who makes it grow?
Who makes it beautiful?
Who wrote the recipe
for our genes,
who has the right
to change it?
Whom should we thank
for our firewood and food,
and in what currency?
Although I was glad
to give up saying grace,
especially in
restaurants, especially
silently, if the people
you were with
didn't pray,
and you tried to sneak
in a quick bow
of the head discreetly
in the middle of
animated conversation,
so as not to interrupt it,
and they reacted
in alarm,
thinking you were
fainting or spilling soup
in your lap
or something,
nevertheless, I miss it
now.
I don't think
the death of one
innocent man

¿Quién lo hace crecer?
¿Quién lo embellece?
¿Quién escribió la receta
de nuestros genes,
quién tiene el derecho
de modificarlos?
¿A quién debemos agradecer
por la leña y la comida,
y con qué moneda?
Aunque me alegra
haber dejado
de dar gracias,
especialmente
en restaurantes, especialmente
en silencio, si la gente
que me acompañaba
no rezaba,
y yo trataba de colar
alguna reverencia furtiva
en mitad
de la animada charla,
con cierta discreción
para no interrumpir
y que no reaccionaran
con alarma,
pensando que estaba por desmayarme
o que había derramado sopa
sobre mi regazo
o algo así,
sin embargo,
lo echo de menos.

two thousand years
ago was an adequate
price for the unreasonable
havoc on resources
we've been enacting
upon the whole world
ever since.
Nor do I think
imitating his suffering
endlessly improves
the account.
Neither do I want
to give up
my first-born
as sacrifice,
neither in battle
nor car chases
nor raves.
Nor do I have fattened
cattle to burn.
I want
to have grandchildren.
I want the world
to exist
and thrive for
and around them
long after I'm gone.
I want to pay
my share of the rent.
I want to live
gratefully
on this bountiful,
generous earth.

No creo que la muerte
de un hombre inocente
hace dos mil años
sea el precio justo
por los irrazonables
estragos que hemos venido
decretando sobre
los recursos del planeta.
Tampoco es que crea
que imitar eternamente
su sufrimiento
mejore nuestra situación.
Tampoco quiero
dar a mi primer hijo
en sacrificio,
en el campo de batalla,
o accidentes automovilísticos,
o *raves*.
Tampoco tengo
ganado de engorda
para sacrificar.
Quiero
tener nietos.
Quiero que el mundo
exista
y prospere
por y alrededor de ellos
mucho después
de que yo haya
partido.
Quiero pagar
mi parte de la renta.

I want to give thanks,
to the right gods
and goddesses,
in the right way,
but I don't know how.
Shouldn't we,
in this age of planetary
ravage
and global sacrifice
of the poor,
and pervasive despair
among the young,
be discussing these
things more?

Quiero vivir
con gratitud
humilde y responsablemente
en este mundo generoso
y pródigo.
Quiero dar gracias
a los dioses y diosas
debidos,
de la forma adecuada,
pero no sé como.
¿No deberíamos,
en esta era de devastación
planetaria y sacrificio global
del pobre, y la aplastante
desesperación de la juventud,
discutir este asunto
con mayor frecuencia?

# Some days he is Van Gogh
*for Philip G*


Part-centaur, part-caesar,
part-troubadour, part-goat,
our man Phil strides
and clambers
up and down the silvery
stone-studded
oregano-scented hills
of Valparaíso and Mojácar,
ferocious in curiosity
and strength.
No one can keep up with him.
He is the happy wanderer,
his knapsack on his back,
canvas and easel in his pack.
In his large hands
the world is street-corner,
is marketplace, is garden,
an intimate encounter in a bar,
a riot of movement
in swift shades of grey.
Some days he is Picasso.
Some days he is Van Gogh.
Some days he's still a kid,
Mom, where do I want to go?
Some days he's Bobby Dylan,
buffeted by wind.
Some days the village
sings to him, the song of
fountains, the song
of the mountain, the deep
lonely song of the sea.

## Algunos días es Van Gogh
*a Philip G*


Parte centauro, parte césar,
parte trovador, parte cabra,
nuestro muchacho Phil
da grandes zancadas
furioso, pleno de curiosidad
y fuerza,
trepa de arriba abajo las plateadas
colinas de piedras engarzadas
y bálsamo de orégano
de Valparaíso y Mojácar.
Nadie puede con él.
Feliz vagabundo,
lienzos y caballete
a cuestas.
En sus enormes manos
el mundo es una esquina callejera,
un mercado, un jardín,
un encuentro íntimo en la cantina,
rebelión de tonos grises
en veloz movimiento.
Algunos días es Picasso.
Algunos días es Van Gogh.
Algunos días es todavía un niño.
¿Mamá, hacia dónde quiero ir?
Algunos días es Bob Dylan,
zarandeado por el viento.
Algunos días la aldea
le canta, la canción de las fuentes,
la canción de la montaña,
la canción profunda
y solitaria del mar.

Some days he is a bee,
lighting on this and that
flower, kitten, nest, lizard,
spider, cactus, *muchacha,*
branch, ready to sting or
make honey.  Tough
and sweet.

Algunos días es una abeja,
posándose sobre esto y aquello,
flor, gatito, nido, lagartija,
araña, cacto, muchacha,
rama; presta para atacar o
hacer miel.  Algunos días es
severo y gentil.

# Sea song, river song

In the dream
the sea became
a river,
and the war
a storm
that killed 800.
I stepped into
the glittering blue
river sea water
and dove
into the current.
My arms hit
a rock, smooth,
and white:
an arm, attached
to a shoulder,
a neck, a torso,
a head.
I stood up
in the shallow water
in alarm.
It was a perfectly
intact woman's
body, white,
like weathered
marble.
Her arms reached
out toward
her companions,
a man, dark brown,
perfect,
intact like her,
and a child.

## Canción de mar, canción de río

En el sueño
el mar se volvió
río,
y la guerra
una tormenta
que mató a 800.
Me adentré en las
luminosas aguas azules
del río mar
dejándome llevar
por la corriente.
Mis brazos golpearon
una roca, tersa,
y blanca,
un brazo, unido
a un hombro,
un cuello, un torso,
una cabeza.
Alarmada
me puse de pie
en las aguas bajas.
Era el cuerpo
de una mujer
perfecto e intacto,
blanco como mármol curtido.
Sus brazos
se abrían
hacia sus compañeros,
un hombre moreno,
perfecto,
intacto como ella,
y un niño.

Then I saw
there were dozens
of bodies
like theirs in the water,
red, black, brown,
naked,
shining, well preserved.
The sunlight
shimmered in waves
over their watery
flesh.
Trees' leaves drifted
slowly across them.
Homer was right:
death is beautiful,
and the body
fallen
in acts of adventure
and daring
the most beautiful.
And what is sand,
if not the accumulated
bones
of the drowned,
ground down
through the pounding
of the sea's waves
to exquisite
miniature stones,
glistening like glass
on the shore,
on which we frolic.

Entonces me di cuenta
que había docenas
de cuerpos
como los suyos bajo el agua,
rojos, negros, cafés,
desnudos,
relucientes, bien preservados.
Los rayos del sol
brillaban trémulos como olas
sobre los cuerpos
acuosos.
Las hojas de los árboles naufragaban
lentamente hacia ellos.
Homero tenía razón:
la muerte es hermosa,
y los cuerpos caídos
en actos de aventura
y valentía
son aun más hermosos.
Y qué es la arena,
sino los huesos
acumulados
de los ahogados,
pulverizados,
por el vaivén
de las olas
convertidos
en piedras pequeñísimas
y exquisitas
relampagueantes como trocitos de vidrio,
en las costas
donde jugueteamos.

Drive your cart and oxen
exuberantly
over the bones
of the dead, Blake said.
But Homer
was wrong about
how to acquire death's
beauty most efficiently,
aggression
adding lifetimes of hatred
and misunderstanding
and clean up
to the mix.
The more afraid we are
of death,
it seems, the more attracted
we are to violence,
as if stealing
another's spirit
would increase the efficacy
of our own
instead of diminishing
and crumbling it.
Sand is beautiful, and drifting
leaves, bleached bones
and polished
many-coloured stones.
You were, you are,
beautiful, dear friends,
both living and dead.

Conduce pletórico
tu buey y tu carreta
sobre los huesos
de los muertos, dijo Blake.
Pero Homero se equivocó
respecto a cómo
conseguir la belleza
de la muerte
de manera más eficiente:
agresión,
añada toda una vida de odio
y malos entendidos
y limpie
la mezcla.
Cuanto más tememos
a la muerte
más nos atrae
la violencia,
como si al robar otro
espíritu estuviésemos
corrigiendo el propio
en lugar de destruirlo
y hacerlo pedazos.
La arena es hermosa, también las hojas
sin rumbo, y los huesos blanqueados
y pulidos
piedritas de colores.
Ustedes eran, son,
hermosos, mis queridos amigos,
ambos muertos y vivos.

I am standing
on the shore
of the world's grave,
I am waving
at you
across the room,
the galaxy,
your spirit bones
shine in the river,
sea, street,
sky,
this tender vale,
most beautifully.

Estoy parada
en la orilla
de la tumba del mundo,
y os saludo
a través del cuarto,
la galaxia,
los huesos de vuestros espíritus
brillan hermosamente
en el río,
el mar, la calle,
el cielo,
este tierno valle.

## Gracias

As for me, *amigos*,
I have been supremely
happy here with you,
walking through
the green-misted *vegas*
of Mojácar
in these magical days,
lifted out of time,
on the edge of our lives
and the deep singing sea,
threading our way
between steep rock and
fragrant herb, and
stately eucalyptus,
stirred today by exhilarating
high wind.
Here endeth a seven-
thousand-year-old Ugaritic
enchantment.
Here riseth a golden tree.
Last night the lights
went out in the city
on the hill.
Everything became still.
In the distance
we heard gypsy guitars,
quivering,
Federico García Lorca,
inconsolable,
weeping in the dark.
Oil lamps flickered
from caves.
*Sí, poetas, amigos,*
*pintores,*

## Gracias

Yo, amigos,
he sido sumamente
feliz aquí entre ustedes
caminando por la verde neblina
de los valles de Mojácar
en estos mágicos días
fuera del tiempo
a orillas de nuestras vidas
y del profundo canto
del mar
tramando nuestros pasos
entre los ásperos riscos,
la aromática hierba
y el majestuoso eucalipto,
provocado
por un viento excitante.
Aquí terminan
los siete mil años
del hechizo ugarítico.
Aquí crece el árbol dorado.
Anoche las luces
se apagaron en la ciudad
dejando a oscuras la colina.
Todo quedó inmóvil.
En la distancia  se escuchó
un temblor de guitarras gitanas,
Federico García Lorca,
inconsolable,
lamentándose en la oscuridad.
En las cuevas parpadeaban
las linternas.
Sí, poetas, amigos,
pintores,

I found joy, here,
blooming, jasmine-scented,
in the desert,
in these fields of sorrow,
this land of "death
without eyes and of arrows."
This valley
of the shadow of the heart,
where the world
begins
and ends,
and begins again,
among bulrushes, rustling,
under the watchful
dark staring red gaze
of the old *bruja*
in the ravine,
sung to by cicadas,
who are happy, *amigos*,
as we are, as we have been,
who are "drunk
with light,"
and know the secret
of the "birth of grass"
and blue sky and blood
and the night.

aquí encontré la felicidad
floreciendo, con perfume de jazmín,
en el desierto,
en estos campos de pena
tierra de la "muerte sin ojos
y las flechas."
Este valle
sombra del corazón
donde el mundo
comienza
y termina,
y vuelve a comenzar,
entre los juncos del barranco,
susurrando, bajo la mirada rojiza
vigilante
profunda y fija
de la vieja bruja,
arrullado por las cigarras,
que son felices, amigos,
como lo somos nosotros,
como lo hemos sido,
cigarras, "borrachas
de luz,"
que conocen el secreto
del "origen de la hierba"
y el cielo azul y la sangre
y la noche.

# Notes

"Désir, désir qui sait…" René Char, "La bibliothèque est en feu," *La bibliothèque est en feu et autres poèmes* (Paris: GLM, 1957), 14-16: 16; transl. into English by John Thompson, *John Thompson: Collected Poems and Translations*, ed. Peter Sanger (Fredericton, NB: Goose Lane, 1995), 181-184: 184.

Ghazal 1: "My hands that used to be heartshaped fluttering leaves/have become thick roots, gnarled in soil." Dorothy Livesay, "Disasters of the Sun," *Disasters of the Sun* (Burnaby, BC: Blackfish,1971), and set to music by Barbara Pentland (UManitoba Archives, Reel-to-Reel Tapes 1965-1973, Box 2, Tape 11, 1977).

Ghazal 5: "Dachau farmyards." Leonard Cohen, *Beautiful Losers* (Toronto: M&S, 1966). "Brainless chickie nobs, crafty pigoons." Margaret Atwood, *Oryx and Crake* (Toronto/Montreal: M&S, 2003).

Ghazal 6: "Our mouths are wet with blood: is it the blood we'll live by?" John Thompson, "Stilt Jack," Ghazal XV, *John Thompson: Collected Poems and Translations*, 121.

Ghazal 8: "From bitter searching of the heart,/we rise to play a greater part." F.R. Scott, "Villanelle for Our Time," *Overture* (Toronto: Ryerson, 1945); performed by Leonard Cohen on his 2003 CD recording, *Dear Heather* (Old Ideas LLC /BMI, 2004), with background vocals by Anjani Thomas. The text appears on his website, at www.leonardcohen.com.

Ghazal 9: "I river, I river, I river." Erin Mouré, "Gorgeous," *Furious* (Toronto: Anansi, 1988), 79-80: 80.

"Welding and other joining procedures" appeared on the Canadian Association of Physics website on the 100th anniversary of Einstein's death in 2005, at www.cap.ca and in *Rampike*, 25th Anniversary Edition II (January 2006).

"Optimistic thoughts" considers an idea suggested by American writer and shaman Martín Prechtel, among others, that from the point of view of traditional indigenous practices, with their numerous seasonal rituals and gestures of sacrifice whose purpose is to ensure gratitude and care in the use of resources, the doctrine of the substitutionary sacrifice of Christ appears to represent a "blank cheque" for modern cultures, cancelling in advance our pervasive human sense of dependency and ongoing debt to the earth and larger cosmos, and attendant need for rites of compensation and accountability. Margaret Atwood's essay, *Payback: Debt and the Shadow Side of Wealth* (Toronto: Anansi, 2008), considers a similar idea. The last stanza of the sequence is from Jovette Marchessault's visionary novel, *Des caillous blancs pour les forêts obscures* (Montréal: Leméac, 1974), 38, transl. as *White Pebbles in the Dark Forests*, by Yvonne M. Klein (Vancouver: Talonbooks, 1990), 28-29.

The last stanza of "The Late Evening News" is adapted from Rainer Maria Rilke's *Letters*, cited in J.B. Leishman's Introduction to *Rilke: Selected Poems*, transl. Leishman (London: Penguin, 1964), 21. With thanks to J.S. Porter.

"Accidents, all accidents" recalls David McPhail's picture book, *Those Terrible Toy-Breakers* (New York: Parents Magazine Press, 1980).

*Mennonitische geistliche Lieder*. Original lyrics are cited here (unless otherwise indicated) from the revised North American edition of *Gesangbuch der Mennoniten* (1942): Hymn 1: #397 *Nun ruhen alle Wälder*, Paul Gerhardt (d. 1676); #406 *So fliehen unsre Tage hin!* author unknown; #405 *Müde bin ich, geh zur Ruh*, Luise Hensel (d. 1876). Hymn 2: #385 *Wach auf, mein Herz, und singe*, Paul Gerhardt (d. 1676); #384 *Dein treues Aug hat mich bewacht*, after Johannes Friedrich Möckel (d. 1729). Hymn 3: #471 *Aus dem Himmel ferne*, Wilhelm Hey (d. 1854); #472 *Weil ich Jesu Schäflein bin*, Luise von Hayn (d. 1782). Hymn 4: #421 *Des Jahres schöner Schmuck entweicht*, Viktor Friedrich von Strauss und Torney (d. 1899); #304 *Herr, bleib bei mir*, English lyrics H.F. Lyte (d. 1847), German transl. Ida Sulzberger (n.d.). Hymn 5: #307 *Schönster Herr Jesu*, author unknown (Münster, 1677). Hymn 6: #331 *Näher, mein Gott, zu Dir*, English lyrics Sara Flower Adams (d. 1848), German transl. Erhardt Friedrich Wunderlich (d. 1895); #111 *Herz und Herz vereint zusammen*, N.L. Graf von Zinzendorf (d. 1760); *Wenn ich ein Vöglein wär*, German folksong. Hymn 7: #91 *Du Sonne der Gerechtigkeit*, Christian Gottlieb Göz (d. 1803). Hymn 8: #495 *Geht nun hin und grabt mein Grab*, Ernst Moritz Arndt (d. 1860). Hymn 9: *Wann ekj mol groot sie*, German folktale, translated here from English into the original Plautdietsch by Erica Ens. Hymn 10: *This world is not my home*, 19th c. American gospel song, S.D. Burton (d. 1892). Hymn 11: #71 *O Haupt voll Blut und Wunden*, Paul Gerhardt (d. 1676). Hymn 12: #73 *O Du Liebe meiner Liebe*, author unknown. *Gesangbuch der Mennoniten*, Rosthern, Saskatchewan: Allgemeine Konferenz der Mennonitengemeinschaft Nordamerikas, 1942.

I thank Erin Mouré for teaching me to trans(e)late my trilingual heritage with greater élan: the women in my family sang these hymns, and a thousand others, cheerfully, all day, every day, while milking the cows, shelling the peas, washing the dishes and putting the children to bed, generously interspersed with humorously inflected folksongs and folktales in Plautdietsch, our indigenous mothertongue. We sang these hymns in church as well, several times a week, in lusty four-part harmonies. They are singing in me now.

"The alarm clock invented the day." Leonard Cohen, "The Pure List and the Commentary," *Flowers for Hitler* (Toronto/Montreal: M&S, 1964, 1970), 89-90: 90.

"Death pangs/turned the room/iridescent/at five in the afternoon." Federico García Lorca, *Lament for Ignacio Sánchez Mejías,* transl. Alan S. Trueblood, *Federico García Lorca: Selected Verse,* ed. Christopher Maurer (New York: Farrar Straus Giroux), 261-273: 273.

"Tonal cruelty,/cultural condescension/and malice." Scott Hightower, "Undependable," *Part of the Bargain* (Washington: Copper Canyon Press, 2005), 11.

"Granules of sugar/on a boy's lip." Scott Hightower, "Dildo Lob," *Part of the Bargain,* 13.

رغبـة المغـرب والشـرق/The envy of Occident and Orient." "*Raghbatal maghribi/wa sharq.*/La envidia de Oriente /y Occidente." With thanks to Abdella Abdou for advice on the Arabic transcription of an emir's magnificent royal boast during the era of the Moorish reign over Granada, still extant on the poetically inscribed wall of the Alhambra's *Patio de los Arrayanes* ("Court of the Myrtles").

"death/without eyes/and of arrows." Federico García Lorca, "Thamar and Amnon," transl. Stephen Spender and J.L. Gili, *The Selected Poems of Federico García Lorca,* ed. Francisco García Lorca and Donald M. Allen, Introduction by W.S. Merwin (New York: New Directions, 2005), 101-105: 101.

"drunk with light." "From *Poem of the* Soleá," 35-36: 35; "the birth of grass." "¡Cicada!" 9-13: 9. *Federico García Lorca: Selected Verse: A Bilingual Edition,* Vol. 3, ed. Christopher Maurer, transl. Francisco Aragon, et al (New York: Farrar, Straus and Giroux, 1989, 1994).

Some of these poems have appeared in *Review: Literature and Arts of the Americas* (UK), Atlas (UK), *Fourth River (US),* Open Letter, Prairie Fire, *Rampike, Contemporary Verse 2, Voices from Oodena* (WIWF, 2006), *71 Poems* for *George Bowering*, ed. Jean Baird (ECW Press, 2006), *A/Cross Sections: New Manitoba Writing*, ed. Katherine Bitney and Andris Taskans (Winnipeg, MB: Manitoba Writers' Guild, 2007), *The Heart Does Break: Canadian Writers on Grief and Mourning* (Random House, 2009), "Poetry on the Buses" (Windsor, ON: The Green Corridor, 2005), "Poetry in Motion" (Winnipeg, MB: Manitoba Writers' Guild, 2006), and in *Autorettrato* (Spain), with Spanish translation by María Clara Calvo Burgos.

# Acknowledgements

Thank you to The Canada Council for the Arts, The Manitoba Arts Council, The Manitoba Writers' Guild and Artspace (Winnipeg, Manitoba), The Canada Research Chair Council (Ottawa), b.h. Yael (Toronto), University of Windsor (Ontario), Brandon University (Manitoba), Fundación Valparaíso (Spain) and Deep Bay Artist Residency (Manitoba), for graciously providing travel funds, writing time and space.

Thank you to Israel García Montero of Madrid for the cover image. Thank you to the team at Turnstone Press for grace, imaginative empathy and hard work, in turning our multilingual manuscript into a beautiful book.

*Available from Turnstone Press*
*poetry by Di Brandt*

questions i asked my mother
Agnes in the Sky
Jerusalem, beloved